50 Food Food Recipes for Home

By: Kelly Johnson

Table of Contents

- Classic Cheeseburger
- Spicy Chicken Sandwich
- Crispy Chicken Tenders
- Beef Tacos
- Loaded Nachos
- Bacon Cheeseburger Fries
- Chicken Quesadillas
- Double Cheeseburger
- BBQ Pulled Pork Sandwiches
- Fish Tacos
- Onion Rings
- Mozzarella Sticks
- Sweet and Sour Chicken
- Chicken Wings
- Loaded Potato Skins
- Breakfast Burritos
- Philly Cheesesteak
- Sloppy Joes
- Veggie Burgers
- Chili Cheese Fries
- Chicken Parmesan Sandwich
- Beef Sliders
- Garlic Fries
- Buffalo Chicken Dip
- Classic Hot Dogs
- Crispy Fish Sandwich
- Stuffed Crust Pizza
- Breakfast Sandwiches
- Beef Burritos
- Cheese Stuffed Meatballs
- Chicken Nuggets
- Stuffed Jalapeno Poppers

- Grilled Cheese Sandwiches
- Beef and Bean Chili
- Soft Pretzels
- Chicken Caesar Wraps
- Teriyaki Chicken Bowls
- Cheeseburger Pizza
- BBQ Chicken Pizza
- Meatball Subs
- Breakfast Skillet
- Taco Salad
- Potato Wedges
- Buffalo Wings with Blue Cheese Dip
- Chicken Fajitas
- Pepperoni Pizza Rolls
- Garlic Parmesan Chicken Wings
- Sausage and Peppers Sandwiches
- Chicken and Waffles
- Classic Clam Chowder

Classic Cheeseburger

Ingredients:

- **For the Patties:**
    - 1 lb ground beef (80% lean)
    - 1/2 tsp salt
    - 1/2 tsp black pepper
    - 1/2 tsp garlic powder (optional)
    - 1/2 tsp onion powder (optional)
- **For Assembly:**
    - 4 hamburger buns
    - 4 slices of cheddar cheese
    - Lettuce leaves
    - Tomato slices
    - Pickles
    - Ketchup
    - Mustard
    - Mayonnaise (optional)

Instructions:

1. **Prepare the Patties:**
    - In a bowl, gently mix the ground beef with salt, pepper, garlic powder, and onion powder.
    - Divide the mixture into 4 equal portions and shape each into a patty, about 3/4 inch thick.
    - Use your thumb to make a small indentation in the center of each patty to help prevent bulging.
2. **Cook the Patties:**
    - Preheat your grill or a skillet over medium-high heat.
    - Cook the patties for about 3-4 minutes per side, or until they reach your desired level of doneness.
    - Place a slice of cheese on each patty during the last minute of cooking and cover to melt.
3. **Toast the Buns:**
    - While the patties are cooking, lightly butter the insides of the hamburger buns.
    - Toast the buns on a skillet or grill until golden brown.
4. **Assemble the Cheeseburgers:**
    - Spread ketchup, mustard, and mayonnaise on the bottom half of each bun.
    - Place a lettuce leaf on each bun, followed by a tomato slice and pickles.
    - Add the cooked cheeseburger patty.
    - Top with the other half of the bun.

5. **Serve:**
    - Serve immediately with your favorite sides like fries or chips.

Enjoy your delicious Classic Cheeseburger!

Spicy Chicken Sandwich

Ingredients:

- **For the Chicken:**
    - 4 boneless, skinless chicken breasts
    - 1 cup buttermilk
    - 1 large egg
    - 1 cup all-purpose flour
    - 1/2 cup cornstarch
    - 2 tsp paprika
    - 1 tsp cayenne pepper
    - 1 tsp garlic powder
    - 1 tsp onion powder
    - 1 tsp salt
    - 1/2 tsp black pepper
    - Vegetable oil (for frying)
- **For the Sauce:**
    - 1/2 cup mayonnaise
    - 2 tbsp hot sauce (adjust to taste)
    - 1 tbsp honey
    - 1/2 tsp smoked paprika
- **For Assembly:**
    - 4 hamburger buns
    - Lettuce leaves
    - Tomato slices
    - Pickles (optional)

Instructions:

1. **Prepare the Chicken:**
    - Flatten the chicken breasts to an even thickness using a meat mallet or rolling pin. This helps them cook evenly.
    - In a bowl, mix the buttermilk and egg. Place the chicken breasts in the mixture, ensuring they are fully submerged. Marinate in the refrigerator for at least 30 minutes, or up to 4 hours.
2. **Prepare the Coating:**
    - In a shallow dish, whisk together flour, cornstarch, paprika, cayenne pepper, garlic powder, onion powder, salt, and black pepper.
    - Remove each chicken breast from the buttermilk mixture and dredge in the flour mixture, pressing lightly to coat evenly.
3. **Fry the Chicken:**

- Heat about 1 inch of vegetable oil in a large skillet over medium-high heat until it reaches 350°F (175°C).
- Fry the chicken breasts in batches (don't overcrowd the pan) for about 5-7 minutes per side, or until golden brown and cooked through. The internal temperature should reach 165°F (74°C). Drain on paper towels.

4. **Prepare the Sauce:**
   - In a small bowl, combine mayonnaise, hot sauce, honey, and smoked paprika. Mix well and adjust seasoning to taste.

5. **Assemble the Sandwiches:**
   - Toast the hamburger buns if desired.
   - Spread a generous amount of spicy sauce on the bottom half of each bun.
   - Place a lettuce leaf, a tomato slice, and pickles (if using) on top.
   - Add the fried chicken breast on top of the vegetables.
   - Spread more spicy sauce on the top bun and place it on top of the sandwich.

6. **Serve:**
   - Serve immediately with your favorite sides like fries or coleslaw.

Enjoy your Spicy Chicken Sandwich!

Crispy Chicken Tenders

Ingredients:

- **For the Chicken:**
  - 1 lb chicken tenders or chicken breasts, cut into strips
  - 1 cup buttermilk
  - 1 large egg
- **For the Breading:**
  - 1 cup all-purpose flour
  - 1 cup breadcrumbs (plain or panko)
  - 1/2 cup grated Parmesan cheese (optional)
  - 1 tsp paprika
  - 1 tsp garlic powder
  - 1 tsp onion powder
  - 1/2 tsp salt
  - 1/2 tsp black pepper
  - 1/2 tsp dried oregano (optional)
  - 1/2 tsp dried thyme (optional)
- **For Frying:**
  - Vegetable oil (for frying)

Instructions:

1. **Marinate the Chicken:**
   - In a bowl, mix the buttermilk and egg.
   - Add the chicken tenders to the mixture and marinate for at least 30 minutes, or up to 4 hours in the refrigerator.
2. **Prepare the Breading:**
   - In a shallow dish or bowl, combine flour, breadcrumbs, Parmesan cheese (if using), paprika, garlic powder, onion powder, salt, black pepper, oregano, and thyme.
   - Mix well.
3. **Bread the Chicken:**
   - Remove each chicken tender from the buttermilk mixture, allowing excess to drip off.
   - Dredge the chicken tenders in the breadcrumb mixture, pressing lightly to coat evenly.
4. **Fry the Chicken:**
   - Heat about 1 inch of vegetable oil in a large skillet over medium-high heat until it reaches 350°F (175°C).

- Fry the chicken tenders in batches (don't overcrowd the pan) for about 4-5 minutes per side, or until golden brown and cooked through. The internal temperature should reach 165°F (74°C).
- Drain on paper towels or a wire rack.
5. **Serve:**
    - Serve immediately with your favorite dipping sauces such as honey mustard, barbecue sauce, or ranch dressing.

Enjoy your crispy and delicious chicken tenders!

Beef Tacos

Ingredients:

- **For the Beef Filling:**
    - 1 lb ground beef
    - 1 small onion, finely chopped
    - 2 cloves garlic, minced
    - 1 packet taco seasoning mix (or homemade, see below)
    - 1/2 cup water
    - 1 tbsp olive oil (if needed)
- **For Homemade Taco Seasoning (optional):**
    - 1 tbsp chili powder
    - 1 tsp paprika
    - 1 tsp ground cumin
    - 1/2 tsp garlic powder
    - 1/2 tsp onion powder
    - 1/2 tsp dried oregano
    - 1/4 tsp cayenne pepper (optional)
    - 1/2 tsp salt
    - 1/4 tsp black pepper
- **For Assembly:**
    - 8 small taco shells or tortillas
    - Shredded lettuce
    - Diced tomatoes
    - Shredded cheddar cheese
    - Sour cream
    - Salsa or pico de gallo
    - Sliced jalapeños (optional)
    - Fresh cilantro (optional)

Instructions:

1. **Prepare the Beef Filling:**
    - Heat olive oil in a large skillet over medium heat (if needed).
    - Add chopped onion and cook until softened, about 3-4 minutes.
    - Add minced garlic and cook for another 30 seconds.
    - Add ground beef and cook until browned, breaking it up with a spoon, about 5-7 minutes. Drain excess fat if necessary.
2. **Season the Beef:**
    - Sprinkle the taco seasoning mix (or homemade seasoning) over the browned beef.
    - Stir well to coat the beef evenly.

- Pour in the water and simmer for 5 minutes, or until the mixture thickens and becomes well combined.
3. **Prepare the Toppings:**
    - While the beef is cooking, prepare your taco toppings: shred the lettuce, dice the tomatoes, shred the cheese, and set out sour cream, salsa, and any other desired toppings.
4. **Warm the Taco Shells:**
    - Heat taco shells or tortillas according to package instructions, usually in the oven or microwave.
5. **Assemble the Tacos:**
    - Spoon the beef mixture into each taco shell or tortilla.
    - Top with shredded lettuce, diced tomatoes, shredded cheese, and any other desired toppings like sour cream or salsa.
    - Garnish with fresh cilantro or sliced jalapeños if desired.
6. **Serve:**
    - Serve immediately with your favorite side dishes like Mexican rice or refried beans.

Enjoy your flavorful beef tacos!

Loaded Nachos

Ingredients:

- **For the Nachos:**
    - 1 bag (about 12 oz) tortilla chips
    - 1 lb ground beef or chicken (or a mix of both)
    - 1 small onion, finely chopped
    - 2 cloves garlic, minced
    - 1 packet taco seasoning mix (or homemade, see below)
    - 1/2 cup water
    - 1 cup shredded cheddar cheese
    - 1 cup shredded Monterey Jack cheese
    - 1 can (15 oz) black beans, drained and rinsed
    - 1 cup canned or fresh sliced jalapeños (optional)
    - 1 cup salsa or pico de gallo
- **For Homemade Taco Seasoning (optional):**
    - 1 tbsp chili powder
    - 1 tsp paprika
    - 1 tsp ground cumin
    - 1/2 tsp garlic powder
    - 1/2 tsp onion powder
    - 1/2 tsp dried oregano
    - 1/4 tsp cayenne pepper (optional)
    - 1/2 tsp salt
    - 1/4 tsp black pepper
- **For Toppings:**
    - 1 cup sour cream
    - 1/2 cup chopped fresh cilantro
    - 1 avocado, diced or guacamole
    - 1 cup diced tomatoes
    - Sliced green onions (optional)

Instructions:

1. **Prepare the Meat:**
    - In a large skillet over medium heat, cook the ground beef or chicken with the chopped onion until the meat is browned and the onion is softened, about 5-7 minutes.
    - Add minced garlic and cook for an additional 30 seconds.
    - Sprinkle the taco seasoning mix (or homemade seasoning) over the meat and stir to combine.
    - Pour in the water and simmer for about 5 minutes, until the mixture thickens.

2. **Prepare the Nachos:**
    - Preheat your oven to 375°F (190°C).
    - On a large baking sheet or oven-safe dish, spread out a layer of tortilla chips.
    - Evenly distribute the cooked meat over the chips.
    - Sprinkle black beans and sliced jalapeños (if using) over the meat.
    - Sprinkle the shredded cheddar and Monterey Jack cheese evenly over the top.
3. **Bake the Nachos:**
    - Place the baking sheet or dish in the preheated oven and bake for about 10 minutes, or until the cheese is melted and bubbly.
4. **Add Toppings:**
    - Remove the nachos from the oven and immediately top with salsa or pico de gallo.
    - Add dollops of sour cream, diced avocado or guacamole, chopped cilantro, diced tomatoes, and sliced green onions if desired.
5. **Serve:**
    - Serve immediately while the nachos are warm and the cheese is gooey.

Enjoy your delicious and loaded nachos!

Bacon Cheeseburger Fries

Ingredients:

- **For the Fries:**
    - 4 cups frozen French fries (or homemade fries, see note below)
    - 1-2 tbsp vegetable oil (if needed)
- **For the Toppings:**
    - 1/2 lb ground beef
    - 1 small onion, finely chopped
    - 2 cloves garlic, minced
    - 1 packet taco seasoning mix (or homemade, see below)
    - 1/2 cup water
    - 1 cup shredded cheddar cheese
    - 1/2 cup cooked bacon, crumbled
    - 1 cup diced tomatoes
    - 1/4 cup pickles, chopped
    - 1/2 cup shredded lettuce
- **For Homemade Taco Seasoning (optional):**
    - 1 tbsp chili powder
    - 1 tsp paprika
    - 1 tsp ground cumin
    - 1/2 tsp garlic powder
    - 1/2 tsp onion powder
    - 1/2 tsp dried oregano
    - 1/4 tsp cayenne pepper (optional)
    - 1/2 tsp salt
    - 1/4 tsp black pepper
- **For Serving:**
    - Ketchup
    - Mustard
    - Mayonnaise (optional)

Instructions:

1. **Prepare the Fries:**
    - Cook the frozen French fries according to the package instructions until crispy. If using homemade fries, bake or fry them until golden and crispy.
    - If needed, toss the fries with a little vegetable oil before baking or frying for extra crispiness.
2. **Prepare the Beef:**

- In a large skillet over medium heat, cook the ground beef with chopped onion until browned and cooked through, about 5-7 minutes. Drain excess fat if necessary.
- Add minced garlic and cook for an additional 30 seconds.
- Stir in the taco seasoning mix (or homemade seasoning) and water. Simmer for about 5 minutes until the mixture thickens.

3. **Assemble the Fries:**
    - Preheat your oven to 375°F (190°C) if you need to melt the cheese.
    - On a large baking sheet or oven-safe dish, spread the cooked fries in an even layer.
    - Evenly distribute the seasoned ground beef over the fries.
    - Sprinkle the shredded cheddar cheese evenly over the beef.
4. **Bake the Fries:**
    - Place the baking sheet or dish in the preheated oven and bake for about 5-7 minutes, or until the cheese is melted and bubbly.
5. **Add the Toppings:**
    - Remove from the oven and immediately top with crumbled bacon, diced tomatoes, chopped pickles, and shredded lettuce.
6. **Serve:**
    - Serve immediately with ketchup, mustard, and mayonnaise on the side if desired.

Enjoy your indulgent Bacon Cheeseburger Fries!

Chicken Quesadillas

Ingredients:

- **For the Chicken:**
    - 1 lb boneless, skinless chicken breasts
    - 1 tbsp olive oil
    - 1 tsp ground cumin
    - 1 tsp paprika
    - 1/2 tsp garlic powder
    - 1/2 tsp onion powder
    - 1/2 tsp chili powder
    - 1/2 tsp salt
    - 1/4 tsp black pepper
- **For the Quesadillas:**
    - 4 large flour tortillas
    - 2 cups shredded cheddar cheese
    - 1 cup shredded Monterey Jack cheese
    - 1/2 cup finely chopped bell peppers (any color)
    - 1/2 cup finely chopped onions
    - 1/2 cup fresh cilantro, chopped (optional)
- **For Serving (optional):**
    - Sour cream
    - Salsa or pico de gallo
    - Guacamole

Instructions:

1. **Prepare the Chicken:**
    - Preheat your grill or skillet over medium-high heat.
    - Rub the chicken breasts with olive oil and season with cumin, paprika, garlic powder, onion powder, chili powder, salt, and black pepper.
    - Grill or cook the chicken in the skillet for about 6-8 minutes per side, or until fully cooked and the internal temperature reaches 165°F (74°C).
    - Let the chicken rest for a few minutes before slicing or shredding it.
2. **Prepare the Quesadillas:**
    - Heat a large skillet over medium heat.
    - Place one tortilla in the skillet and sprinkle half of the cheddar and Monterey Jack cheeses evenly over the tortilla.
    - Add a layer of chicken, chopped bell peppers, and onions on top of the cheese.
    - Sprinkle the remaining cheese over the chicken and vegetables.
    - Place a second tortilla on top to form a sandwich.
3. **Cook the Quesadillas:**

- Cook the quesadilla for about 2-3 minutes on each side, or until the tortillas are golden brown and the cheese is melted. You may need to press down gently with a spatula to ensure even cooking.
- Remove from the skillet and let cool slightly before cutting into wedges.
4. **Serve:**
    - Serve warm with sour cream, salsa, or guacamole on the side.

Enjoy your delicious Chicken Quesadillas!

Double Cheeseburger

Ingredients:

- **For the Patties:**
    - 1 lb ground beef (80% lean)
    - 1/2 tsp salt
    - 1/2 tsp black pepper
    - 1/2 tsp garlic powder (optional)
    - 1/2 tsp onion powder (optional)
- **For Assembly:**
    - 4 hamburger buns
    - 4 slices cheddar cheese
    - 4 slices American cheese
    - Lettuce leaves
    - Tomato slices
    - Pickles
    - Ketchup
    - Mustard
    - Mayonnaise (optional)
    - 4 slices cooked bacon (optional)

Instructions:

1. **Prepare the Patties:**
    - In a bowl, gently mix the ground beef with salt, pepper, garlic powder, and onion powder.
    - Divide the mixture into 8 equal portions and shape each portion into a patty, about 3/4 inch thick.
    - Use your thumb to make a small indentation in the center of each patty to help prevent bulging.
2. **Cook the Patties:**
    - Preheat your grill or a skillet over medium-high heat.
    - Cook the patties for about 3-4 minutes per side, or until they reach your desired level of doneness. For double cheeseburgers, cook until medium to medium-well.
    - During the last minute of cooking, place a slice of cheddar cheese on each patty and cover to melt. Repeat with the American cheese if you like double layers of cheese.
3. **Toast the Buns:**
    - While the patties are cooking, lightly butter the insides of the hamburger buns.
    - Toast the buns on a skillet or grill until golden brown.
4. **Assemble the Double Cheeseburgers:**
    - Spread ketchup, mustard, and mayonnaise on the bottom half of each bun.

        - Place a lettuce leaf, a tomato slice, and pickles on top.
        - Add two patties with melted cheese on top of the vegetables.
        - If using, place a slice of cooked bacon on top of the patties.
        - Spread additional ketchup, mustard, or mayonnaise on the top bun and place it on top of the burger.
5. **Serve:**
        - Serve immediately with your favorite sides like fries or onion rings.

Enjoy your hearty Double Cheeseburger!

BBQ Pulled Pork Sandwiches

Ingredients:

- **For the Pulled Pork:**
    - 3-4 lbs pork shoulder (also known as pork butt)
    - 1 tbsp paprika
    - 1 tbsp brown sugar
    - 1 tsp garlic powder
    - 1 tsp onion powder
    - 1 tsp ground cumin
    - 1/2 tsp salt
    - 1/2 tsp black pepper
    - 1/2 tsp cayenne pepper (optional, for extra heat)
    - 1 cup BBQ sauce (store-bought or homemade, see note below)
    - 1 cup chicken or beef broth
    - 1 onion, quartered
    - 3 cloves garlic, smashed
- **For the Coleslaw (optional but recommended):**
    - 4 cups shredded cabbage (green and/or red)
    - 1 cup shredded carrots
    - 1/2 cup mayonnaise
    - 2 tbsp apple cider vinegar
    - 1 tbsp sugar
    - Salt and pepper to taste
- **For Assembly:**
    - 8 hamburger buns
    - Extra BBQ sauce for serving

Instructions:

1. **Prepare the Pork:**
    - In a small bowl, mix paprika, brown sugar, garlic powder, onion powder, cumin, salt, black pepper, and cayenne pepper (if using).
    - Rub the spice mixture all over the pork shoulder.
    - Place the pork shoulder in a slow cooker. Add the quartered onion and smashed garlic around the pork.
    - Pour the chicken or beef broth over the pork.
    - Cover and cook on low for 8-10 hours, or until the pork is very tender and easily shreds with a fork.
2. **Shred the Pork:**
    - Once the pork is cooked, remove it from the slow cooker and place it on a cutting board. Discard the bones and excess fat.

- Shred the pork using two forks or your hands. Return the shredded pork to the slow cooker and stir in the BBQ sauce. Cook on low for an additional 30 minutes to allow the flavors to meld.
3. **Prepare the Coleslaw (optional):**
    - In a large bowl, combine shredded cabbage and carrots.
    - In a small bowl, whisk together mayonnaise, apple cider vinegar, sugar, salt, and pepper.
    - Pour the dressing over the cabbage mixture and toss to coat evenly. Refrigerate until ready to serve.
4. **Assemble the Sandwiches:**
    - Toast the hamburger buns if desired.
    - Spoon a generous amount of BBQ pulled pork onto the bottom half of each bun.
    - Top with coleslaw if desired.
    - Drizzle extra BBQ sauce over the pork if you like.
    - Place the top half of the bun on the sandwich.
5. **Serve:**
    - Serve immediately with your favorite sides like baked beans, fries, or corn on the cob.

Enjoy your flavorful BBQ Pulled Pork Sandwiches!

Fish Tacos

Ingredients:

- **For the Fish:**
    - 1 lb white fish fillets (such as cod, tilapia, or halibut)
    - 1 cup all-purpose flour
    - 1 tsp paprika
    - 1 tsp garlic powder
    - 1/2 tsp onion powder
    - 1/2 tsp cayenne pepper (optional)
    - 1/2 tsp salt
    - 1/2 tsp black pepper
    - 1 cup buttermilk
    - Vegetable oil (for frying)
- **For the Slaw:**
    - 4 cups shredded cabbage (green or red or a mix)
    - 1/2 cup shredded carrots
    - 1/4 cup chopped fresh cilantro
    - 1/4 cup mayonnaise
    - 2 tbsp lime juice
    - 1 tbsp honey
    - 1/2 tsp salt
    - 1/4 tsp black pepper
- **For Assembly:**
    - 8 small tortillas (corn or flour)
    - 1 avocado, sliced
    - 1/2 cup crumbled queso fresco or shredded cheese
    - Lime wedges (for garnish)

Instructions:

1. **Prepare the Fish:**
    - In a shallow dish, mix together flour, paprika, garlic powder, onion powder, cayenne pepper, salt, and black pepper.
    - Dip each fish fillet into the buttermilk, allowing excess to drip off.
    - Dredge the fish in the seasoned flour mixture, pressing lightly to coat.
    - Heat about 1 inch of vegetable oil in a large skillet over medium-high heat until it reaches 350°F (175°C).
    - Fry the fish fillets in batches for about 3-4 minutes per side, or until golden brown and cooked through. Drain on paper towels.
2. **Prepare the Slaw:**

    - In a large bowl, combine shredded cabbage, shredded carrots, and chopped cilantro.
    - In a small bowl, whisk together mayonnaise, lime juice, honey, salt, and black pepper.
    - Pour the dressing over the cabbage mixture and toss to coat evenly.
3. **Warm the Tortillas:**
    - Heat the tortillas in a dry skillet over medium heat or wrap them in foil and warm them in the oven.
4. **Assemble the Tacos:**
    - Place a few pieces of fried fish in the center of each tortilla.
    - Top with a generous amount of slaw.
    - Add avocado slices and crumbled queso fresco or shredded cheese.
    - Garnish with lime wedges.
5. **Serve:**
    - Serve immediately with additional lime wedges and your favorite side dishes.

Enjoy your delicious and fresh Fish Tacos!

Onion Rings

Ingredients:

- **For the Onion Rings:**
    - 2 large onions (such as yellow or sweet onions)
    - 1 cup all-purpose flour
    - 1/2 tsp salt
    - 1/2 tsp black pepper
    - 1 tsp paprika
    - 1 tsp garlic powder
    - 1 cup buttermilk (or milk with 1 tbsp lemon juice added)
    - 1 cup breadcrumbs (panko or regular)
    - Vegetable oil (for frying)

Instructions:

1. **Prepare the Onions:**
    - Peel the onions and slice them into 1/4-inch thick rings. Separate the rings and set aside.
2. **Prepare the Breading:**
    - In a shallow dish, mix together flour, salt, black pepper, paprika, and garlic powder.
    - In another shallow dish, pour the buttermilk (or milk with lemon juice).
    - In a third shallow dish, place the breadcrumbs.
3. **Bread the Onion Rings:**
    - Dredge each onion ring in the seasoned flour mixture, shaking off excess.
    - Dip the floured ring into the buttermilk, allowing excess to drip off.
    - Coat the ring with breadcrumbs, pressing lightly to adhere. Repeat with all onion rings.
4. **Fry the Onion Rings:**
    - Heat about 1-2 inches of vegetable oil in a large skillet or deep fryer to 350°F (175°C).
    - Fry the onion rings in batches, being careful not to overcrowd the pan, for about 2-3 minutes per side, or until golden brown and crispy.
    - Remove the onion rings with a slotted spoon and drain on paper towels.
5. **Serve:**
    - Serve immediately with your favorite dipping sauces, such as ketchup, ranch, or aioli.

Enjoy your crispy, golden onion rings!

Mozzarella Sticks

Ingredients:

- **For the Mozzarella Sticks:**
    - 12 oz mozzarella cheese sticks (about 12 sticks)
    - 1 cup all-purpose flour
    - 2 large eggs
    - 1 cup breadcrumbs (plain or Italian, or a mix of panko and regular)
    - 1/2 cup grated Parmesan cheese (optional)
    - 1 tsp garlic powder
    - 1 tsp dried oregano
    - 1/2 tsp salt
    - 1/2 tsp black pepper
    - Vegetable oil (for frying)
- **For Serving:**
    - Marinara sauce or ranch dressing

Instructions:

1. **Prepare the Cheese:**
    - Cut the mozzarella cheese sticks in half if you prefer shorter sticks or leave them whole. Place them in the freezer for about 30 minutes to firm up. This helps them hold their shape during frying.
2. **Prepare the Breading:**
    - In a shallow dish, place the flour.
    - In another shallow dish, beat the eggs.
    - In a third shallow dish, mix together the breadcrumbs, Parmesan cheese (if using), garlic powder, dried oregano, salt, and black pepper.
3. **Bread the Mozzarella Sticks:**
    - Dredge each mozzarella stick in flour, shaking off excess.
    - Dip it into the beaten eggs, allowing excess to drip off.
    - Coat it with the breadcrumb mixture, pressing gently to ensure an even coating.
    - For extra crunch, repeat the egg and breadcrumb coating process for a double layer.
4. **Fry the Mozzarella Sticks:**
    - Heat about 2 inches of vegetable oil in a deep skillet or fryer to 350°F (175°C).
    - Fry the mozzarella sticks in batches, without overcrowding, for about 1-2 minutes or until golden brown and crispy. Be careful not to overcook as the cheese can melt out.
    - Remove with a slotted spoon and drain on paper towels.
5. **Serve:**
    - Serve immediately with marinara sauce or ranch dressing for dipping.

Enjoy your crispy, cheesy mozzarella sticks!

Sweet and Sour Chicken

Ingredients:

- **For the Chicken:**
    - 1 lb boneless, skinless chicken breasts or thighs, cut into bite-sized pieces
    - 1/2 cup all-purpose flour
    - 1/2 cup cornstarch
    - 1/2 tsp salt
    - 1/2 tsp black pepper
    - 1 large egg, beaten
    - 1 cup vegetable oil (for frying)
- **For the Sweet and Sour Sauce:**
    - 1/2 cup rice vinegar
    - 1/2 cup granulated sugar
    - 1/4 cup ketchup
    - 2 tbsp soy sauce
    - 1 tbsp cornstarch mixed with 2 tbsp water (slurry)
    - 1/4 cup pineapple juice (optional for extra flavor)
- **For the Vegetables (optional):**
    - 1 cup bell peppers, cut into chunks (any color)
    - 1 cup pineapple chunks (fresh or canned)
    - 1/2 cup onion, cut into chunks
- **For Garnish (optional):**
    - Sesame seeds
    - Chopped green onions

Instructions:

1. **Prepare the Chicken:**
    - In a bowl, mix together flour, cornstarch, salt, and black pepper.
    - Dip each piece of chicken into the beaten egg, then dredge it in the flour mixture, pressing lightly to coat.
    - Heat vegetable oil in a large skillet or wok over medium-high heat until it reaches 350°F (175°C).
    - Fry the chicken in batches, without overcrowding the pan, for about 4-5 minutes or until golden brown and cooked through. Remove with a slotted spoon and drain on paper towels.
2. **Prepare the Sweet and Sour Sauce:**
    - In a medium saucepan, combine rice vinegar, sugar, ketchup, soy sauce, and pineapple juice (if using).
    - Bring to a simmer over medium heat, stirring occasionally.

- Once the mixture begins to simmer, stir in the cornstarch slurry and continue to cook until the sauce thickens, about 1-2 minutes. Remove from heat.
3. **Prepare the Vegetables (if using):**
    - In the same skillet used for frying the chicken, add a little oil if needed and sauté bell peppers, onion, and pineapple chunks over medium heat for 2-3 minutes until just tender.
4. **Combine:**
    - Add the fried chicken back to the skillet with the vegetables.
    - Pour the sweet and sour sauce over the chicken and vegetables, tossing to coat evenly and heat through.
5. **Serve:**
    - Garnish with sesame seeds and chopped green onions if desired.
    - Serve hot over steamed rice or noodles.

Enjoy your flavorful Sweet and Sour Chicken!

Chicken Wings

Ingredients:

- **For the Chicken Wings:**
    - 2 lbs chicken wings (drumettes and flats separated)
    - 1 tbsp olive oil
    - 1/2 tsp salt
    - 1/2 tsp black pepper
    - 1/2 tsp garlic powder
    - 1/2 tsp onion powder
    - 1/2 tsp paprika
- **For the Sauce (optional, see variations below):**
    - 1/2 cup buffalo sauce (or hot sauce of choice)
    - 1/4 cup melted butter
    - 1 tbsp honey (optional, for a touch of sweetness)

Instructions:

1. **Prepare the Wings:**
    - Preheat your oven to 400°F (200°C) or preheat a deep fryer to 375°F (190°C).
    - Pat the chicken wings dry with paper towels. This helps them get crispy.
    - In a large bowl, toss the wings with olive oil, salt, black pepper, garlic powder, onion powder, and paprika until evenly coated.
2. **Bake or Fry the Wings:**
   To Bake:
    - Arrange the wings in a single layer on a baking sheet lined with parchment paper or a wire rack (for extra crispiness).
    - Bake for 40-45 minutes, flipping halfway through, until the wings are golden brown and crispy.
3. **To Fry:**
    - Heat vegetable oil in a deep fryer or large pot to 375°F (190°C).
    - Fry the wings in batches, without overcrowding the pot, for about 8-10 minutes, or until golden brown and crispy.
    - Remove the wings with a slotted spoon and drain on paper towels.
4. **Prepare the Sauce:**
    - If using buffalo sauce: In a small bowl, mix together buffalo sauce, melted butter, and honey (if using).
    - Heat the sauce in a saucepan over low heat until warmed through.
5. **Toss the Wings:**
    - Place the cooked wings in a large bowl.
    - Pour the sauce over the wings and toss to coat evenly.
6. **Serve:**

    - Serve the wings hot with celery sticks and your favorite dipping sauces, such as ranch or blue cheese dressing.

Variations:

- **Garlic Parmesan Wings:** Toss cooked wings with melted butter, minced garlic, and grated Parmesan cheese.
- **Honey BBQ Wings:** Toss cooked wings with a mixture of BBQ sauce and honey.
- **Lemon Pepper Wings:** Toss cooked wings with lemon zest, cracked black pepper, and melted butter.

Enjoy your crispy, flavorful chicken wings!

Loaded Potato Skins

Ingredients:

- **For the Potato Skins:**
    - 4 large russet potatoes
    - 2 tbsp olive oil
    - 1/2 tsp salt
    - 1/4 tsp black pepper
- **For the Toppings:**
    - 1 cup shredded cheddar cheese
    - 1/2 cup cooked bacon, crumbled
    - 1/4 cup chopped green onions
    - 1/2 cup sour cream
- **For Garnish (optional):**
    - Extra chopped green onions
    - Extra sour cream

Instructions:

1. **Prepare the Potatoes:**
    - Preheat your oven to 400°F (200°C).
    - Wash and scrub the potatoes. Pat them dry.
    - Prick each potato with a fork a few times. Rub with olive oil and sprinkle with salt.
    - Place the potatoes directly on the oven rack and bake for 45-60 minutes, or until tender. Alternatively, you can bake them on a baking sheet.
2. **Scoop Out the Flesh:**
    - Let the potatoes cool slightly after baking. Slice them in half lengthwise.
    - Use a spoon to scoop out most of the potato flesh, leaving about 1/4-inch of potato around the skin. Save the scooped-out potato flesh for another use, like mashed potatoes.
3. **Crisp the Potato Skins:**
    - Increase the oven temperature to 425°F (220°C).
    - Brush the inside of each potato skin with a little more olive oil. Place the skins cut-side up on a baking sheet.
    - Bake for 10 minutes, flip the skins, and bake for another 5 minutes until the edges are crispy.
4. **Add Toppings:**
    - Sprinkle shredded cheddar cheese evenly into the crispy potato skins.
    - Return to the oven and bake for an additional 5 minutes, or until the cheese is melted and bubbly.
    - Remove from the oven and sprinkle with crumbled bacon and chopped green onions.

5. **Serve:**
    - Serve the loaded potato skins warm with a dollop of sour cream on top or on the side.
    - Garnish with additional green onions and sour cream if desired.

Enjoy your crispy and flavorful Loaded Potato Skins!

Breakfast Burritos

Ingredients:

- **For the Filling:**
    - 1 lb breakfast sausage (or chorizo, bacon, or ham)
    - 6 large eggs
    - 1/4 cup milk
    - 1 cup shredded cheddar cheese (or your favorite cheese)
    - 1 cup diced potatoes (hash browns or pre-cooked)
    - 1 cup diced bell peppers (any color)
    - 1/2 cup diced onions
    - 1 tbsp olive oil
    - Salt and pepper to taste
- **For Assembly:**
    - 6 large flour tortillas
    - 1/4 cup chopped fresh cilantro (optional)
    - Salsa, avocado, or sour cream (for serving)

Instructions:

1. **Prepare the Filling:**
    - In a large skillet, cook the breakfast sausage over medium heat until fully cooked and browned, breaking it up into crumbles. Remove the sausage from the skillet and set aside. Drain excess fat if necessary.
    - In the same skillet, add olive oil and sauté the diced onions and bell peppers until softened, about 5 minutes. Add the diced potatoes and cook until heated through or slightly crispy. Season with salt and pepper. Set aside.
    - In a bowl, whisk together eggs and milk. Pour into the skillet and cook over medium heat, stirring occasionally, until the eggs are scrambled and cooked through. Add the cooked sausage back to the skillet and stir to combine.
2. **Assemble the Burritos:**
    - Warm the flour tortillas in a dry skillet or microwave to make them more pliable.
    - Lay out a tortilla on a flat surface. Spoon a portion of the egg mixture in the center of the tortilla.
    - Sprinkle with shredded cheese and add any optional toppings like chopped cilantro.
    - Fold in the sides of the tortilla, then roll up the bottom edge tightly to form a burrito. Repeat with the remaining tortillas and filling.
3. **Heat the Burritos (optional):**
    - For a crispy exterior, heat a skillet over medium heat. Place the burritos seam-side down and cook for 2-3 minutes per side, or until golden and crispy.
4. **Serve:**

- Serve the breakfast burritos warm with salsa, avocado, and/or sour cream on the side.

Make-Ahead Tips:

- **Freezing:** To make ahead, assemble the burritos and wrap each tightly in foil or plastic wrap. Freeze for up to 3 months. To reheat, unwrap and microwave for 1-2 minutes, or bake in a preheated oven at 375°F (190°C) for 20-25 minutes.

Enjoy your hearty and satisfying Breakfast Burritos!

Philly Cheesesteak

Ingredients:

- **For the Cheesesteak:**
    - 1 lb ribeye steak (or sirloin), thinly sliced
    - 1 tbsp vegetable oil
    - 1 large onion, thinly sliced
    - 1 green bell pepper, thinly sliced (optional)
    - 1 cup mushrooms, sliced (optional)
    - 4-6 hoagie rolls or sub rolls
    - 8 slices provolone cheese (or American cheese)
    - Salt and pepper to taste
- **For the Marinade (optional but recommended):**
    - 2 tbsp soy sauce
    - 1 tbsp Worcestershire sauce
    - 1 tsp garlic powder
    - 1/2 tsp onion powder
    - 1/2 tsp black pepper

Instructions:

1. **Prepare the Steak:**
    - **Optional Marinade:** In a bowl, mix soy sauce, Worcestershire sauce, garlic powder, onion powder, and black pepper. Add the thinly sliced steak and toss to coat. Let it marinate for at least 15 minutes, or up to 1 hour if you have time.
    - If not marinating, season the steak slices with a bit of salt and pepper.
2. **Cook the Vegetables:**
    - Heat 1 tbsp vegetable oil in a large skillet or cast-iron pan over medium heat.
    - Add the onions and cook until they begin to soften, about 5 minutes.
    - Add the bell pepper and mushrooms (if using) and cook until tender and caramelized, about 5-7 more minutes. Remove vegetables from the skillet and set aside.
3. **Cook the Steak:**
    - In the same skillet, add a bit more oil if necessary and increase the heat to high.
    - Add the thinly sliced steak to the hot skillet. Cook, stirring occasionally, until the steak is browned and cooked through, about 3-5 minutes. Season with additional salt and pepper to taste.
4. **Combine:**
    - Return the cooked onions, bell pepper, and mushrooms to the skillet with the steak. Stir to combine and heat through.
5. **Assemble the Sandwiches:**
    - Preheat your oven broiler (if toasting the rolls).

- Split the hoagie rolls and place them on a baking sheet, cut side up.
- Place 2 slices of cheese on each roll and toast under the broiler until the cheese is melted and bubbly, about 1-2 minutes. Watch closely to avoid burning.
- Divide the steak and vegetable mixture among the rolls.

6. **Serve:**
    - Serve the Philly Cheesesteaks hot, with extra condiments like hot peppers or ketchup if desired.

Enjoy your authentic and delicious Philly Cheesesteak!

Sloppy Joes

Ingredients:

- **For the Sloppy Joes:**
    - 1 lb ground beef (80% lean)
    - 1 small onion, finely chopped
    - 1 small bell pepper, finely chopped (any color)
    - 2 cloves garlic, minced
    - 1 cup ketchup
    - 1/4 cup tomato paste
    - 2 tbsp brown sugar
    - 1 tbsp Worcestershire sauce
    - 1 tbsp apple cider vinegar
    - 1 tsp mustard (yellow or Dijon)
    - 1/2 tsp smoked paprika
    - 1/4 tsp cayenne pepper (optional, for heat)
    - Salt and black pepper to taste
    - 4-6 hamburger buns

Instructions:

1. **Cook the Meat:**
    - In a large skillet or saucepan, cook the ground beef over medium-high heat until browned and fully cooked, breaking it up with a spoon as it cooks.
    - Remove excess fat if necessary.
2. **Add Vegetables:**
    - Add the chopped onion, bell pepper, and garlic to the skillet with the beef. Cook until the vegetables are softened, about 5 minutes.
3. **Prepare the Sauce:**
    - Stir in the ketchup, tomato paste, brown sugar, Worcestershire sauce, apple cider vinegar, mustard, smoked paprika, and cayenne pepper (if using).
    - Mix well and let the sauce come to a simmer. Reduce heat to low and simmer for about 10-15 minutes, or until the mixture has thickened to your liking. Stir occasionally.
4. **Season:**
    - Taste and adjust seasoning with salt and black pepper as needed.
5. **Serve:**
    - Toast the hamburger buns if desired.
    - Spoon the sloppy joe mixture onto the bottom half of each bun. Top with the other half of the bun.
6. **Optional Garnishes:**
    - Serve with pickles, coleslaw, or cheese if desired.

Enjoy your hearty and flavorful Sloppy Joes!

Veggie Burgers

Ingredients:

- **For the Veggie Burgers:**
    - 1 can (15 oz) black beans, drained and rinsed
    - 1/2 cup cooked quinoa or brown rice
    - 1/2 cup finely chopped onion
    - 1/2 cup finely chopped bell pepper (any color)
    - 1/2 cup grated carrots
    - 2 cloves garlic, minced
    - 1/2 cup breadcrumbs (regular or panko)
    - 1/4 cup chopped fresh cilantro (or parsley)
    - 1 egg, beaten (or 1 tbsp flaxseed meal mixed with 3 tbsp water for a vegan option)
    - 1 tbsp soy sauce or tamari
    - 1 tsp cumin
    - 1/2 tsp smoked paprika
    - 1/2 tsp salt
    - 1/4 tsp black pepper
    - 2 tbsp olive oil (for cooking)
- **For Serving:**
    - 4-6 hamburger buns
    - Lettuce, tomato slices, pickles, onions, or any desired toppings
    - Ketchup, mustard, or other condiments

Instructions:

1. **Prepare the Mixture:**
    - In a large bowl, mash the black beans with a fork or potato masher until mostly smooth, leaving some chunks for texture.
    - Add the cooked quinoa or brown rice, chopped onion, bell pepper, grated carrots, and minced garlic. Mix well.
2. **Combine Ingredients:**
    - Stir in the breadcrumbs, chopped cilantro, beaten egg (or flaxseed mixture), soy sauce, cumin, smoked paprika, salt, and black pepper. Mix until everything is combined and holds together. If the mixture is too wet, add more breadcrumbs; if too dry, add a little water or additional soy sauce.
3. **Form the Patties:**
    - Divide the mixture into 4-6 equal portions and shape each portion into a patty, about 1/2-inch thick.
4. **Cook the Patties:**
    - Heat olive oil in a large skillet over medium heat.

- Cook the patties for 4-5 minutes per side, or until golden brown and crispy on the outside. Flip carefully using a spatula.
5. **Serve:**
    - Toast the hamburger buns if desired.
    - Place the cooked veggie patties on the buns and top with your choice of lettuce, tomato, pickles, onions, and condiments.

Make-Ahead Tips:

- **Freezing:** You can freeze the uncooked patties. Place them on a baking sheet lined with parchment paper and freeze until solid, then transfer to a freezer bag or container. Cook from frozen, adding a couple of extra minutes to the cooking time.

Enjoy your delicious and satisfying Veggie Burgers!

Chili Cheese Fries

Ingredients:

- **For the Fries:**
    - 4 large russet potatoes
    - 2 tbsp vegetable oil
    - 1/2 tsp salt
    - 1/4 tsp black pepper
    - 1/4 tsp paprika (optional)
- **For the Chili:**
    - 1 lb ground beef or turkey
    - 1 small onion, finely chopped
    - 2 cloves garlic, minced
    - 1 can (15 oz) diced tomatoes
    - 1 can (15 oz) kidney beans, drained and rinsed
    - 1 tbsp chili powder
    - 1 tsp cumin
    - 1/2 tsp paprika
    - 1/2 tsp dried oregano
    - 1/4 tsp cayenne pepper (optional, for heat)
    - Salt and pepper to taste
- **For the Cheese Sauce:**
    - 1 cup shredded cheddar cheese
    - 1/2 cup milk
    - 1 tbsp all-purpose flour
    - 1 tbsp butter
    - 1/4 tsp garlic powder
    - 1/4 tsp onion powder
    - Salt to taste
- **For Garnish (optional):**
    - Chopped green onions
    - Sliced jalapeños
    - Sour cream

Instructions:

1. **Prepare the Fries:**
    - Preheat your oven to 425°F (220°C).
    - Wash and peel the potatoes. Cut them into thin strips or wedges.
    - Toss the potato strips in a large bowl with vegetable oil, salt, pepper, and paprika.

- Spread the fries in a single layer on a baking sheet. Bake for 25-30 minutes, flipping halfway through, until golden brown and crispy. Alternatively, you can use a deep fryer if you prefer.

2. **Prepare the Chili:**
    - In a large skillet or saucepan, cook the ground beef or turkey over medium heat until browned. Drain any excess fat.
    - Add the chopped onion and cook until softened, about 5 minutes. Add the minced garlic and cook for an additional minute.
    - Stir in the diced tomatoes, kidney beans, chili powder, cumin, paprika, dried oregano, and cayenne pepper (if using).
    - Simmer for 15-20 minutes, stirring occasionally, until the chili is thickened. Adjust seasoning with salt and pepper.

3. **Prepare the Cheese Sauce:**
    - In a small saucepan, melt the butter over medium heat. Whisk in the flour and cook for about 1 minute to create a roux.
    - Gradually whisk in the milk, ensuring there are no lumps. Continue to cook, stirring constantly, until the mixture thickens.
    - Remove from heat and stir in the shredded cheddar cheese until melted and smooth. Season with garlic powder, onion powder, and salt to taste.

4. **Assemble the Chili Cheese Fries:**
    - Place the cooked fries on a serving platter or individual plates.
    - Spoon the hot chili over the fries.
    - Drizzle or spoon the cheese sauce on top of the chili.

5. **Garnish and Serve:**
    - Garnish with chopped green onions, sliced jalapeños, or a dollop of sour cream if desired.
    - Serve immediately while the fries and cheese sauce are hot.

Enjoy your hearty and indulgent Chili Cheese Fries!

Chicken Parmesan Sandwich

Ingredients:

- **For the Chicken:**
    - 2 large boneless, skinless chicken breasts
    - 1 cup all-purpose flour
    - 2 large eggs
    - 1 cup breadcrumbs (plain or Italian)
    - 1/2 cup grated Parmesan cheese
    - 1/2 tsp garlic powder
    - 1/2 tsp onion powder
    - 1/2 tsp dried basil
    - 1/2 tsp dried oregano
    - Salt and pepper to taste
    - Vegetable oil (for frying)
- **For the Sandwich:**
    - 4 hoagie rolls or sub rolls
    - 1 cup marinara sauce (store-bought or homemade)
    - 1 cup shredded mozzarella cheese
    - Fresh basil leaves (optional, for garnish)
    - Additional grated Parmesan cheese (optional)

Instructions:

1. **Prepare the Chicken:**
    - Preheat the oven to 375°F (190°C).
    - Place the chicken breasts between two sheets of plastic wrap or parchment paper. Use a meat mallet or rolling pin to pound them to an even thickness, about 1/2 inch.
    - Set up a breading station with three shallow dishes:
        - Dish 1: Flour seasoned with a little salt and pepper.
        - Dish 2: Beaten eggs.
        - Dish 3: Breadcrumbs mixed with grated Parmesan, garlic powder, onion powder, dried basil, dried oregano, salt, and pepper.
    - Dredge each chicken breast in the flour, shaking off excess, then dip in the beaten eggs, and finally coat with the breadcrumb mixture, pressing lightly to adhere.
2. **Fry the Chicken:**
    - Heat a generous amount of vegetable oil in a large skillet over medium-high heat.
    - Fry the chicken breasts for 3-4 minutes per side, or until golden brown and cooked through. The internal temperature should reach 165°F (74°C).
    - Remove the chicken from the skillet and drain on paper towels.

3. **Assemble the Sandwiches:**
    - Spread a thin layer of marinara sauce on each hoagie roll.
    - Place the fried chicken breasts on the rolls.
    - Spoon more marinara sauce over the chicken.
    - Sprinkle shredded mozzarella cheese on top of the sauce.
4. **Bake:**
    - Place the assembled sandwiches on a baking sheet.
    - Bake in the preheated oven for 10-12 minutes, or until the cheese is melted and bubbly, and the rolls are toasted.
5. **Serve:**
    - Garnish with fresh basil leaves and additional grated Parmesan cheese if desired.
    - Serve hot.

Enjoy your crispy and cheesy Chicken Parmesan Sandwich!

Beef Sliders

Ingredients:

- **For the Sliders:**
    - 1 lb ground beef (80% lean)
    - 1/2 cup finely chopped onion
    - 1/4 cup breadcrumbs (optional, for binding)
    - 1 egg (optional, for binding)
    - 1 tbsp Worcestershire sauce
    - 1 tsp garlic powder
    - 1 tsp onion powder
    - 1/2 tsp salt
    - 1/4 tsp black pepper
    - 8 slider buns
    - Cheese slices (optional, for topping)
    - Lettuce, tomato slices, pickles, and other desired toppings
- **For the Sauce (optional):**
    - 1/4 cup mayonnaise
    - 2 tbsp ketchup
    - 1 tbsp mustard
    - 1 tsp pickle relish (optional)

Instructions:

1. **Prepare the Beef Mixture:**
    - In a large bowl, combine the ground beef, chopped onion, breadcrumbs, egg (if using), Worcestershire sauce, garlic powder, onion powder, salt, and pepper. Mix gently until just combined; avoid overmixing to keep the sliders tender.
2. **Form the Patties:**
    - Divide the beef mixture into 8 equal portions and shape each portion into a small patty, about 1/2 inch thick. Use your thumb to make a small indentation in the center of each patty to help them cook evenly.
3. **Cook the Sliders:**
   To Grill:
    - Preheat the grill to medium-high heat.
    - Grill the patties for about 3-4 minutes per side, or until they reach your desired level of doneness. Add cheese slices during the last minute of grilling if you want cheeseburgers.
4. **To Pan-Fry:**
    - Heat a skillet or griddle over medium-high heat.
    - Cook the patties for about 3-4 minutes per side, or until they reach your desired level of doneness. Add cheese slices during the last minute of cooking if desired.

5. **Prepare the Buns:**
   - Lightly toast the slider buns on the grill or in a toaster if desired.
6. **Prepare the Sauce (optional):**
   - In a small bowl, mix together mayonnaise, ketchup, mustard, and pickle relish (if using) until smooth.
7. **Assemble the Sliders:**
   - Spread the sauce on the bottom half of each bun if using.
   - Place a cooked patty on each bun.
   - Top with lettuce, tomato slices, pickles, and any other desired toppings.
   - Cover with the top half of the bun.
8. **Serve:**
   - Serve the beef sliders immediately while hot.

Enjoy your juicy and flavorful Beef Sliders!

Garlic Fries

Ingredients:

- **For the Fries:**
    - 4 large russet potatoes
    - 2-3 tbsp vegetable oil
    - 1/2 tsp salt
    - 1/4 tsp black pepper
- **For the Garlic Butter:**
    - 4 cloves garlic, minced
    - 4 tbsp unsalted butter
    - 1 tbsp olive oil
    - 2 tbsp chopped fresh parsley (or 1 tbsp dried parsley)
    - 1/4 tsp crushed red pepper flakes (optional, for a bit of heat)
    - Additional salt to taste

Instructions:

1. **Prepare the Potatoes:**
    - Wash and peel the potatoes. Cut them into thin strips or wedges, about 1/4 to 1/2 inch thick.
    - Place the cut potatoes in a bowl of cold water and let them soak for at least 30 minutes. This helps to remove excess starch and makes the fries crispier.
2. **Cook the Fries:**
    - Preheat your oven to 425°F (220°C).
    - Drain and pat the potatoes dry with a clean towel.
    - Toss the potatoes with vegetable oil, salt, and black pepper until evenly coated.
    - Spread the potatoes in a single layer on a baking sheet lined with parchment paper or a non-stick baking mat.
    - Bake for 25-30 minutes, flipping halfway through, until the fries are golden brown and crispy. For extra crispiness, you can broil them for the last 2-3 minutes, but watch carefully to prevent burning.
3. **Prepare the Garlic Butter:**
    - While the fries are baking, melt the butter and olive oil together in a small saucepan over medium heat.
    - Add the minced garlic and cook, stirring frequently, until fragrant and lightly golden, about 1-2 minutes. Be careful not to burn the garlic.
    - Remove from heat and stir in the chopped parsley and crushed red pepper flakes (if using). Season with a pinch of additional salt to taste.
4. **Toss the Fries:**
    - Once the fries are done baking, transfer them to a large bowl.
    - Pour the garlic butter mixture over the hot fries and toss gently to coat.

5. **Serve:**
    - Serve the garlic fries hot, garnished with extra parsley if desired.

Enjoy your deliciously garlicky and crispy Garlic Fries!

Buffalo Chicken Dip

Ingredients:

- **For the Dip:**
    - 2 cups cooked chicken, shredded or chopped (rotisserie chicken works great)
    - 1 package (8 oz) cream cheese, softened
    - 1/2 cup sour cream
    - 1/2 cup ranch dressing (or blue cheese dressing if preferred)
    - 1/2 cup buffalo wing sauce (adjust to taste)
    - 1 cup shredded cheddar cheese (or a mix of cheddar and mozzarella)
    - 1/2 cup crumbled blue cheese (optional, for extra flavor)
    - 1/4 cup chopped green onions (optional, for garnish)
- **For Serving:**
    - Tortilla chips, celery sticks, carrot sticks, or crackers

Instructions:

1. **Preheat Oven:**
    - Preheat your oven to 350°F (175°C).
2. **Prepare the Dip Mixture:**
    - In a large bowl, combine the softened cream cheese, sour cream, ranch dressing, and buffalo wing sauce. Mix until smooth.
    - Stir in the shredded chicken, shredded cheddar cheese, and crumbled blue cheese (if using). Mix until everything is well combined.
3. **Bake the Dip:**
    - Transfer the mixture to a baking dish (an 8x8-inch dish works well).
    - Spread it evenly and sprinkle a little extra cheddar cheese on top if desired.
    - Bake in the preheated oven for 20-25 minutes, or until the dip is hot and bubbly, and the cheese is melted and slightly golden.
4. **Garnish and Serve:**
    - Remove from the oven and let it cool slightly.
    - Garnish with chopped green onions if desired.
    - Serve with tortilla chips, celery sticks, carrot sticks, or crackers for dipping.

Enjoy your flavorful and creamy Buffalo Chicken Dip!

Classic Hot Dogs

Ingredients:

- **For the Hot Dogs:**
    - 4 beef hot dogs (or your preferred variety)
    - 4 hot dog buns
    - Mustard (yellow or Dijon)
    - Ketchup (optional)
    - Relish (optional)
- **For Optional Toppings:**
    - Chopped onions
    - Shredded cheddar cheese
    - Sauerkraut
    - Pickles

Instructions:

1. **Prepare the Hot Dogs:**
   To Boil:
    - Fill a saucepan with enough water to cover the hot dogs.
    - Bring the water to a boil.
    - Add the hot dogs to the boiling water and cook for 4-5 minutes, or until heated through.
2. **To Grill:**
    - Preheat your grill to medium-high heat.
    - Place the hot dogs on the grill and cook for about 2-3 minutes per side, or until they have grill marks and are heated through.
3. **To Pan-Fry:**
    - Heat a skillet over medium heat.
    - Add the hot dogs and cook, turning occasionally, for about 5-7 minutes, or until they are evenly browned and heated through.
4. **Toast the Buns (Optional):**
    - For extra flavor and texture, you can lightly toast the hot dog buns.
    - Place the buns cut-side down on the grill or in a toaster oven for 1-2 minutes, or until they are golden brown.
5. **Assemble the Hot Dogs:**
    - Place each cooked hot dog into a toasted bun.
    - Add your preferred condiments such as mustard, ketchup, or relish.
6. **Add Optional Toppings:**
    - Customize your hot dogs with additional toppings like chopped onions, shredded cheddar cheese, sauerkraut, or pickles.
7. **Serve:**

    - Serve the hot dogs immediately while they are warm.

Enjoy your classic hot dogs, perfect for a quick meal or a summer cookout!

Crispy Fish Sandwich

Ingredients:

- **For the Fish:**
    - 4 boneless, skinless fish fillets (such as cod, haddock, or tilapia)
    - 1 cup all-purpose flour
    - 1 tsp paprika
    - 1/2 tsp garlic powder
    - 1/2 tsp onion powder
    - 1/2 tsp salt
    - 1/4 tsp black pepper
    - 1 cup buttermilk
    - 1 cup panko breadcrumbs (for extra crispiness)
    - 1/2 cup cornmeal (optional, for extra crunch)
    - Vegetable oil (for frying)
- **For the Sandwich:**
    - 4 hamburger buns
    - Lettuce leaves
    - Tomato slices
    - Pickles
    - Tartar sauce or mayonnaise (optional)
- **For the Tartar Sauce (optional):**
    - 1/2 cup mayonnaise
    - 2 tbsp chopped dill pickles or pickle relish
    - 1 tbsp lemon juice
    - 1 tsp Dijon mustard
    - 1 tsp chopped fresh parsley (optional)
    - Salt and pepper to taste

Instructions:

1. **Prepare the Fish:**
    - **Set Up Breading Station:** In one bowl, mix together the flour, paprika, garlic powder, onion powder, salt, and pepper. In another bowl, pour the buttermilk. In a third bowl, combine the panko breadcrumbs and cornmeal if using.
    - **Dredge Fish:** Pat the fish fillets dry with paper towels. Dredge each fillet in the seasoned flour, shaking off excess, then dip in the buttermilk, and finally coat with the panko mixture, pressing lightly to adhere.
2. **Fry the Fish:**
    - **Heat Oil:** In a large skillet or deep fryer, heat vegetable oil over medium-high heat to about 350°F (175°C). The oil should be deep enough to cover at least half of the fillets.

- **Cook Fish:** Fry the fish fillets for 3-4 minutes per side, or until golden brown and crispy. The internal temperature should reach 145°F (63°C). Remove the fillets from the oil and drain on paper towels.
3. **Prepare the Tartar Sauce (Optional):**
    - In a small bowl, combine the mayonnaise, chopped pickles or relish, lemon juice, Dijon mustard, and parsley if using. Mix well and season with salt and pepper to taste.
4. **Assemble the Sandwiches:**
    - **Toast Buns:** Lightly toast the hamburger buns if desired.
    - **Build Sandwiches:** Spread tartar sauce or mayonnaise on the bottom half of each bun. Place a lettuce leaf on top, followed by a crispy fish fillet. Add tomato slices and pickles if desired. Top with the other half of the bun.
5. **Serve:**
    - Serve the crispy fish sandwiches immediately while they are hot and crispy.

Enjoy your crunchy and flavorful Crispy Fish Sandwich!

Stuffed Crust Pizza

Ingredients:

- **For the Dough:**
    - 2 1/4 tsp active dry yeast (1 packet)
    - 1 1/2 cups warm water (110°F/45°C)
    - 3 1/2 to 4 cups all-purpose flour
    - 2 tbsp olive oil
    - 1 tsp sugar
    - 1 tsp salt
- **For the Stuffed Crust:**
    - 8 oz string cheese or mozzarella cheese sticks (cut into halves or thirds if needed)
- **For the Pizza:**
    - 1/2 cup pizza sauce
    - 1 1/2 cups shredded mozzarella cheese
    - 1/2 cup shredded cheddar cheese (optional)
    - 1/2 cup sliced pepperoni, cooked sausage, or other toppings (optional)
    - 1/2 cup sliced bell peppers, mushrooms, onions, or other vegetables (optional)
    - 1 tsp dried oregano
    - 1/2 tsp garlic powder
    - 1/4 tsp black pepper
- **For the Garlic Butter (optional):**
    - 2 tbsp unsalted butter, melted
    - 1/2 tsp garlic powder
    - 1/2 tsp dried parsley

Instructions:

1. **Prepare the Dough:**
    - In a small bowl, dissolve the yeast and sugar in warm water. Let it sit for about 5-10 minutes, or until foamy.
    - In a large bowl or stand mixer, combine 3 1/2 cups flour and salt. Make a well in the center and pour in the yeast mixture and olive oil.
    - Mix until a dough forms. If the dough is too sticky, gradually add the remaining flour, 1 tablespoon at a time.
    - Knead the dough on a floured surface for about 5-7 minutes, or until smooth and elastic. You can also knead the dough in the stand mixer with a dough hook attachment for about 5 minutes.
    - Place the dough in a lightly oiled bowl, cover with a damp cloth or plastic wrap, and let it rise in a warm place for 1-1.5 hours, or until doubled in size.
2. **Prepare the Stuffed Crust:**

- Punch down the dough and transfer it to a floured surface. Roll out the dough into a large circle, about 14 inches in diameter.
- Place the string cheese or cheese sticks around the edge of the dough, about 1 inch from the edge.
- Fold the edge of the dough over the cheese and press to seal, creating a stuffed crust.

3. **Assemble the Pizza:**
    - Preheat your oven to 475°F (245°C) and place a pizza stone or an inverted baking sheet inside to heat up.
    - Spread the pizza sauce evenly over the dough, leaving a border around the edges.
    - Sprinkle the shredded mozzarella cheese evenly over the sauce.
    - Add any additional toppings like pepperoni, vegetables, or cooked sausage.
    - Sprinkle dried oregano, garlic powder, and black pepper over the top.
4. **Bake the Pizza:**
    - Transfer the pizza to the preheated pizza stone or baking sheet.
    - Bake for 12-15 minutes, or until the crust is golden brown and the cheese is bubbly and melted.
5. **Prepare the Garlic Butter (Optional):**
    - While the pizza is baking, mix the melted butter, garlic powder, and dried parsley in a small bowl.
    - Brush the garlic butter mixture over the edges of the crust after baking for added flavor.
6. **Serve:**
    - Allow the pizza to cool for a few minutes before slicing.
    - Serve hot and enjoy your delicious Stuffed Crust Pizza!

Enjoy making and eating this cheesy, indulgent Stuffed Crust Pizza!

Breakfast Sandwiches

Ingredients:

- **For the Sandwiches:**
    - 4 large eggs
    - 4 slices of bacon or sausage patties (optional)
    - 4 slices of cheese (American, cheddar, or your preference)
    - 4 English muffins, split and toasted (or your choice of bread or rolls)
    - 1/2 cup spinach or arugula (optional, for a fresh touch)
    - 1 tomato, sliced (optional)
    - 1 avocado, sliced (optional)
- **For the Egg Mixture:**
    - 1/4 cup milk or cream
    - Salt and pepper to taste
    - 1 tbsp butter or oil (for cooking eggs)
- **For the Sauce (optional):**
    - 1/4 cup mayonnaise
    - 1 tbsp Dijon mustard
    - 1 tbsp ketchup
    - 1 tsp hot sauce (optional)

Instructions:

1. **Cook the Bacon or Sausage (Optional):**
    - **Bacon:** In a skillet over medium heat, cook the bacon slices until crispy. Remove and drain on paper towels.
    - **Sausage Patties:** In the same skillet, cook the sausage patties until browned and cooked through. Remove and drain on paper towels.
2. **Prepare the Egg Mixture:**
    - In a bowl, whisk together the eggs, milk or cream, salt, and pepper until well combined.
3. **Cook the Eggs:**
    - Heat butter or oil in a non-stick skillet over medium heat.
    - Pour in the egg mixture and cook, stirring occasionally, until the eggs are scrambled and cooked through. Remove from heat.
4. **Assemble the Sandwiches:**
    - Toast the English muffins or bread of choice.
    - Spread mayonnaise, Dijon mustard, ketchup, and hot sauce (if using) on the cut sides of the toasted muffins or bread.
    - On the bottom half of each muffin or bread, layer the scrambled eggs.
    - Place a slice of cheese on top of the eggs while they are still hot to allow it to melt.

        - Add cooked bacon or sausage patties if using.
        - Top with spinach or arugula, tomato slices, and avocado slices if desired.
        - Cover with the top half of the muffin or bread.
5. **Serve:**
        - Serve the breakfast sandwiches warm.

Enjoy your satisfying and customizable Breakfast Sandwiches!

Beef Burritos

Ingredients:

- **For the Beef Filling:**
    - 1 lb ground beef
    - 1 small onion, finely chopped
    - 2 cloves garlic, minced
    - 1 packet (1 oz) taco seasoning (or use homemade)
    - 1/2 cup tomato sauce or diced tomatoes
    - 1/4 cup water
    - 1/2 cup black beans, drained and rinsed (optional)
    - 1/2 cup corn kernels (optional)
    - Salt and pepper to taste
- **For Assembling the Burritos:**
    - 4 large flour tortillas (10-inch or larger)
    - 1 cup shredded cheddar cheese (or a blend of cheeses)
    - 1/2 cup sour cream
    - 1/2 cup salsa
    - 1/2 cup chopped fresh cilantro (optional)
    - 1 avocado, sliced (optional)
    - Shredded lettuce and diced tomatoes (optional)

Instructions:

1. **Prepare the Beef Filling:**
    - In a large skillet over medium heat, cook the ground beef until browned, breaking it up with a spoon as it cooks. Drain any excess fat.
    - Add the chopped onion and cook until softened, about 3-4 minutes. Stir in the minced garlic and cook for another minute.
    - Stir in the taco seasoning, tomato sauce or diced tomatoes, and water. Mix well and simmer for 5 minutes, or until the mixture is thickened and heated through.
    - Add the black beans and corn, if using. Cook for an additional 2 minutes. Season with salt and pepper to taste. Remove from heat.
2. **Assemble the Burritos:**
    - Warm the flour tortillas in a dry skillet over medium heat or in the microwave to make them more pliable.
    - Lay out each tortilla and spread a small amount of sour cream in the center.
    - Spoon a portion of the beef filling onto the tortilla.
    - Sprinkle shredded cheddar cheese over the beef filling.
    - Add additional toppings such as salsa, chopped cilantro, avocado slices, shredded lettuce, or diced tomatoes if desired.
3. **Roll the Burritos:**

- Fold in the sides of the tortilla over the filling.
- Roll up the tortilla from the bottom, tucking in the sides as you go, to form a tight burrito.
4. **Serve:**
    - Serve the beef burritos immediately, or you can heat them up in a skillet over medium heat to crisp up the outside, if desired.

Enjoy your hearty and flavorful Beef Burritos!

Cheese Stuffed Meatballs

Ingredients:

- **For the Meatballs:**
    - 1 lb ground beef (80% lean)
    - 1/2 lb ground pork (optional, for extra flavor and moisture)
    - 1/2 cup breadcrumbs (plain or Italian)
    - 1/4 cup grated Parmesan cheese
    - 1/4 cup chopped fresh parsley (or 1 tbsp dried parsley)
    - 1 large egg
    - 2 cloves garlic, minced
    - 1 tsp dried oregano
    - 1/2 tsp dried basil
    - 1/2 tsp salt
    - 1/4 tsp black pepper
- **For the Cheese Filling:**
    - 1 cup shredded mozzarella cheese (or provolone, cheddar, or your favorite melting cheese)
- **For the Sauce (optional):**
    - 2 cups marinara sauce (store-bought or homemade)

Instructions:

1. **Prepare the Meatball Mixture:**
    - In a large bowl, combine the ground beef and ground pork (if using).
    - Add the breadcrumbs, grated Parmesan cheese, chopped parsley, egg, minced garlic, dried oregano, dried basil, salt, and pepper.
    - Mix until all ingredients are evenly combined. Avoid over-mixing to keep the meatballs tender.
2. **Form the Meatballs:**
    - Preheat your oven to 375°F (190°C).
    - Take a small amount of the meat mixture and flatten it in your palm. Place about 1 tablespoon of shredded cheese in the center.
    - Gently fold the meat around the cheese and roll it into a ball, making sure the cheese is completely enclosed. Repeat with the remaining meat mixture and cheese.
3. **Cook the Meatballs:**
   To Bake:
    - Place the meatballs on a baking sheet lined with parchment paper or a non-stick baking mat.

- Bake in the preheated oven for 20-25 minutes, or until the meatballs are cooked through and have reached an internal temperature of 160°F (71°C). The cheese inside should be melted.
4. **To Fry:**
    - Heat a few tablespoons of oil in a skillet over medium heat.
    - Add the meatballs and cook, turning occasionally, for about 10-12 minutes, or until browned on all sides and cooked through.
5. **Prepare the Sauce (Optional):**
    - If using marinara sauce, heat it in a saucepan over medium heat until warmed through.
6. **Serve:**
    - If you made the sauce, spoon a bit of sauce onto plates or serving dishes.
    - Place the meatballs on top of the sauce or serve them on their own.
    - Garnish with additional chopped parsley or Parmesan cheese if desired.

Enjoy your Cheese Stuffed Meatballs, perfect as a main dish or an appetizer!

Chicken Nuggets

Ingredients:

- **For the Nuggets:**
    - 1 lb boneless, skinless chicken breasts or thighs, cut into bite-sized pieces
    - 1 cup all-purpose flour
    - 2 large eggs
    - 1 cup breadcrumbs (plain or Italian)
    - 1/2 cup grated Parmesan cheese (optional, for extra flavor)
    - 1 tsp garlic powder
    - 1 tsp onion powder
    - 1/2 tsp paprika
    - 1/2 tsp dried oregano
    - 1/2 tsp salt
    - 1/4 tsp black pepper
    - Vegetable oil (for frying)
- **For Breading (optional):**
    - 1/2 cup buttermilk or milk (for dipping chicken before breading)

Instructions:

1. **Prepare the Chicken:**
    - Cut the chicken breasts or thighs into bite-sized pieces, about 1-2 inches each.
2. **Set Up Breading Stations:**
    - **Flour Station:** Place the flour in a shallow dish. Season with a pinch of salt and pepper.
    - **Egg Mixture:** In a second shallow dish, beat the eggs until well mixed.
    - **Breadcrumb Station:** In a third shallow dish, combine the breadcrumbs, Parmesan cheese (if using), garlic powder, onion powder, paprika, dried oregano, salt, and pepper.
3. **Coat the Chicken:**
    - Dredge each piece of chicken in the flour, shaking off any excess.
    - Dip the floured chicken into the beaten eggs, allowing any excess to drip off.
    - Coat the chicken in the breadcrumb mixture, pressing lightly to ensure the breadcrumbs stick. Place the coated chicken pieces on a plate or baking sheet.
4. **Cook the Nuggets:**
   To Fry:
    - Heat about 1/2 inch of vegetable oil in a large skillet over medium-high heat.
    - Fry the chicken nuggets in batches, being careful not to overcrowd the pan. Cook for 3-4 minutes per side, or until golden brown and crispy, and the internal temperature reaches 165°F (74°C).
    - Remove the cooked nuggets from the oil and drain on paper towels.

5. **To Bake:**
    - Preheat your oven to 400°F (200°C) and line a baking sheet with parchment paper or a non-stick baking mat.
    - Arrange the coated chicken nuggets in a single layer on the baking sheet. Lightly spray or brush with oil.
    - Bake for 15-20 minutes, or until the nuggets are golden brown and the internal temperature reaches 165°F (74°C), flipping halfway through.
6. **Serve:**
    - Serve the chicken nuggets hot with your favorite dipping sauces, such as ketchup, barbecue sauce, honey mustard, or ranch.

Enjoy your homemade Chicken Nuggets!

Stuffed Jalapeno Poppers

Ingredients:

- **For the Poppers:**
    - 12 large jalapeño peppers
    - 8 oz cream cheese, softened
    - 1/2 cup shredded cheddar cheese (or a blend of your choice)
    - 1/4 cup grated Parmesan cheese
    - 1/4 cup cooked and crumbled bacon (optional)
    - 1 tbsp chopped fresh chives or parsley (optional)
    - 1/2 tsp garlic powder
    - 1/2 tsp onion powder
    - Salt and pepper to taste
- **For the Breading (optional):**
    - 1/2 cup all-purpose flour
    - 1 cup breadcrumbs (plain or seasoned)
    - 2 large eggs, beaten
    - Vegetable oil (for frying, if desired)

Instructions:

1. **Prepare the Jalapeños:**
    - Preheat your oven to 375°F (190°C) if baking, or prepare a skillet for frying.
    - Wearing gloves (or using a paper towel), slice each jalapeño in half lengthwise. Remove the seeds and membranes using a spoon or small knife. Be careful not to touch your face, and wash your hands thoroughly afterward.
2. **Make the Filling:**
    - In a bowl, combine the softened cream cheese, shredded cheddar cheese, grated Parmesan cheese, crumbled bacon (if using), chopped chives or parsley, garlic powder, onion powder, salt, and pepper. Mix until smooth and well combined.
3. **Stuff the Jalapeños:**
    - Spoon or pipe the cheese mixture into each jalapeño half, filling generously.
4. **(Optional) Bread the Poppers:**
    - Set up a breading station with three shallow dishes: one with flour, one with beaten eggs, and one with breadcrumbs.
    - Dredge each stuffed jalapeño in flour, shaking off excess, then dip in the beaten eggs, and finally coat with breadcrumbs. Press lightly to ensure the breadcrumbs adhere.
5. **Cook the Poppers:**
    To Bake:

- Arrange the stuffed jalapeños on a baking sheet lined with parchment paper or a non-stick baking mat.
- Bake in the preheated oven for 20-25 minutes, or until the jalapeños are tender and the filling is bubbly and golden.

6. **To Fry:**
   - Heat about 1/2 inch of vegetable oil in a large skillet over medium heat.
   - Fry the stuffed jalapeños in batches, being careful not to overcrowd the pan. Cook for about 2-3 minutes per side, or until golden brown and crispy.
   - Remove the cooked poppers from the oil and drain on paper towels.
7. **Serve:**
   - Serve the stuffed jalapeño poppers hot. They make a great appetizer or snack!

Enjoy your spicy and cheesy Stuffed Jalapeño Poppers!

Grilled Cheese Sandwiches

Ingredients:

- **For the Sandwiches:**
    - 8 slices of bread (white, whole wheat, or your choice)
    - 4 tbsp unsalted butter (softened)
    - 8 oz cheese (such as cheddar, American, Swiss, or a blend of your favorites), sliced or shredded
- **Optional Add-ins:**
    - 4 slices of tomato
    - 4 slices of cooked bacon
    - 1/4 cup caramelized onions
    - 1/4 cup cooked spinach or sautéed mushrooms

Instructions:

1. **Prepare the Bread:**
    - Spread a thin layer of softened butter on one side of each slice of bread. This will help achieve a golden and crispy crust.
2. **Assemble the Sandwiches:**
    - Place the cheese slices or shredded cheese on the unbuttered side of half of the bread slices. If using add-ins like tomato, bacon, or caramelized onions, layer them on top of the cheese.
    - Top with the remaining bread slices, buttered side up, to form sandwiches.
3. **Grill the Sandwiches:**
   To Grill:
    - Heat a non-stick skillet or griddle over medium heat.
    - Place the sandwiches in the skillet (you may need to cook them in batches).
    - Cook for 2-4 minutes per side, or until the bread is golden brown and crispy, and the cheese is melted. Press down lightly with a spatula to ensure even grilling.
4. **To Cook Evenly:**
    - If the bread is browning too quickly before the cheese melts, lower the heat slightly and cover the skillet with a lid for a minute or two to help the cheese melt through.
5. **Serve:**
    - Remove the sandwiches from the skillet and let them cool for a minute before slicing.
    - Serve warm, optionally with a side of tomato soup or your favorite dipping sauce.

Enjoy your delicious and classic Grilled Cheese Sandwiches!

Beef and Bean Chili

Ingredients:

- **For the Chili:**
    - 1 lb ground beef (80% lean)
    - 1 large onion, chopped
    - 2 cloves garlic, minced
    - 1 bell pepper, chopped (any color)
    - 1 can (14.5 oz) diced tomatoes
    - 1 can (15 oz) tomato sauce
    - 1 can (15 oz) kidney beans, drained and rinsed
    - 1 can (15 oz) black beans, drained and rinsed
    - 1 can (15 oz) pinto beans, drained and rinsed
    - 1 cup beef broth
    - 2 tbsp chili powder
    - 1 tsp ground cumin
    - 1/2 tsp smoked paprika (optional, for a smoky flavor)
    - 1/2 tsp dried oregano
    - 1/4 tsp cayenne pepper (optional, for extra heat)
    - Salt and black pepper to taste
- **Optional Garnishes:**
    - Shredded cheddar cheese
    - Sour cream
    - Sliced green onions
    - Chopped fresh cilantro
    - Diced avocado
    - Crushed tortilla chips

Instructions:

1. **Cook the Beef:**
    - In a large pot or Dutch oven, cook the ground beef over medium heat, breaking it up with a spoon as it cooks. Cook until browned and cooked through, about 5-7 minutes. Drain excess fat if necessary.
2. **Add Vegetables:**
    - Add the chopped onion, garlic, and bell pepper to the pot. Cook for about 5 minutes, or until the vegetables are softened and the onion is translucent.
3. **Add Spices:**
    - Stir in the chili powder, ground cumin, smoked paprika (if using), dried oregano, and cayenne pepper (if using). Cook for 1-2 minutes to allow the spices to bloom and become fragrant.
4. **Add Beans and Liquids:**

- Add the diced tomatoes, tomato sauce, kidney beans, black beans, pinto beans, and beef broth to the pot. Stir to combine.
5. **Simmer the Chili:**
    - Bring the mixture to a boil. Reduce the heat to low and let it simmer, uncovered, for at least 30 minutes, or up to 1 hour, stirring occasionally. This allows the flavors to meld and the chili to thicken. Adjust seasoning with salt and pepper to taste.
6. **Serve:**
    - Ladle the chili into bowls and garnish with your choice of toppings such as shredded cheddar cheese, sour cream, sliced green onions, chopped cilantro, diced avocado, or crushed tortilla chips.

Enjoy your rich and comforting Beef and Bean Chili!

Soft Pretzels

Ingredients:

- **For the Dough:**
    - 1 1/2 cups warm water (110°F/45°C)
    - 1 packet (2 1/4 tsp) active dry yeast
    - 1 tbsp granulated sugar
    - 4 cups all-purpose flour
    - 1 tsp salt
    - 2 tbsp unsalted butter, melted
- **For Boiling:**
    - 10 cups water
    - 2/3 cup baking soda
- **For Topping:**
    - Coarse sea salt or pretzel salt
    - 1 egg, beaten (for egg wash)
- **Optional:**
    - 1/4 cup melted butter (for brushing after baking)

Instructions:

1. **Prepare the Dough:**
    - In a large bowl, combine the warm water and sugar. Sprinkle the yeast over the top and let it sit for 5 minutes until foamy.
    - Add the flour, salt, and melted butter to the yeast mixture. Stir until a dough forms.
    - Turn the dough out onto a lightly floured surface and knead for about 5-7 minutes, or until smooth and elastic. You can also use a stand mixer with a dough hook for this step.
2. **Let the Dough Rise:**
    - Place the dough in a lightly oiled bowl, turning it once to coat all sides with oil. Cover the bowl with a damp cloth or plastic wrap and let it rise in a warm, draft-free place for 1 hour, or until doubled in size.
3. **Preheat Oven:**
    - Preheat your oven to 425°F (220°C). Line two baking sheets with parchment paper or silicone baking mats.
4. **Shape the Pretzels:**
    - Punch down the risen dough and divide it into 8 equal pieces.
    - Roll each piece into a long rope, about 18-24 inches long. Shape each rope into a pretzel shape by forming a U with the dough, then crossing the ends over each other and pressing them down onto the bottom of the U to form the pretzel shape.

5. **Boil the Pretzels:**
   - In a large pot, bring the 10 cups of water and baking soda to a boil.
   - Carefully drop a few pretzels into the boiling water (don't overcrowd) and cook for about 30 seconds, turning them halfway through. Use a slotted spoon to remove the pretzels and place them on the prepared baking sheets.
6. **Prepare for Baking:**
   - Brush the boiled pretzels with the beaten egg and sprinkle with coarse sea salt or pretzel salt.
7. **Bake:**
   - Bake in the preheated oven for 12-15 minutes, or until the pretzels are deep golden brown.
8. **Optional Butter Brush:**
   - If desired, brush the hot pretzels with melted butter for extra flavor and a shiny finish.
9. **Serve:**
   - Let the pretzels cool slightly before serving. Enjoy them warm with mustard, cheese sauce, or your favorite dipping sauce!

Enjoy your freshly baked soft pretzels!

Chicken Caesar Wraps

Ingredients:

- **For the Chicken:**
    - 2 cups cooked chicken breast, shredded or diced (grilled or rotisserie chicken works well)
    - 1 tbsp olive oil
    - 1/2 tsp garlic powder
    - 1/2 tsp onion powder
    - 1/2 tsp dried oregano
    - Salt and black pepper to taste
- **For the Wraps:**
    - 4 large flour tortillas or wraps
    - 1 cup romaine lettuce, chopped
    - 1/2 cup grated Parmesan cheese
    - 1/2 cup croutons, slightly crushed (optional, for extra crunch)
- **For the Caesar Dressing:**
    - 1/2 cup Caesar salad dressing (store-bought or homemade)
    - 1 tbsp lemon juice (optional, for extra tang)

Instructions:

1. **Prepare the Chicken:**
    - In a bowl, combine the shredded or diced chicken with olive oil, garlic powder, onion powder, dried oregano, salt, and pepper. Toss to coat evenly.
    - If the chicken is not already cooked, you can sauté it in a skillet over medium heat until cooked through, about 5-7 minutes. If using pre-cooked chicken, simply mix it with the seasonings and heat it if desired.
2. **Prepare the Caesar Dressing:**
    - In a small bowl, mix the Caesar salad dressing with lemon juice if using. This adds a bit of brightness to the dressing.
3. **Assemble the Wraps:**
    - Lay out the tortillas or wraps on a flat surface.
    - Spread a thin layer of Caesar dressing down the center of each tortilla.
    - Layer the chopped romaine lettuce over the dressing.
    - Add the seasoned chicken on top of the lettuce.
    - Sprinkle with grated Parmesan cheese and croutons if using.
4. **Wrap and Serve:**
    - Fold in the sides of the tortilla and then roll it up tightly from the bottom to form a wrap.
    - Cut each wrap in half diagonally for easier eating.
5. **Optional:**

- If desired, you can toast the wraps in a skillet over medium heat for 1-2 minutes on each side to warm them up and make them slightly crispy.

Enjoy your Chicken Caesar Wraps! They make a great lunch or quick dinner option.

Teriyaki Chicken Bowls

Ingredients:

- **For the Teriyaki Chicken:**
  - 1 lb boneless, skinless chicken thighs or breasts, cut into bite-sized pieces
  - 1 tbsp olive oil
  - Salt and pepper to taste
- **For the Teriyaki Sauce:**
  - 1/2 cup soy sauce (low-sodium preferred)
  - 1/4 cup mirin or rice vinegar
  - 1/4 cup brown sugar or honey
  - 2 tbsp cornstarch mixed with 2 tbsp water (for thickening)
  - 2 cloves garlic, minced
  - 1 tbsp fresh ginger, grated or minced
  - 1 tbsp sesame oil (optional)
- **For the Bowls:**
  - 2 cups cooked white or brown rice (or cauliflower rice for a low-carb option)
  - 1 cup broccoli florets (steamed or roasted)
  - 1/2 cup shredded carrots
  - 1/2 cup snap peas or bell peppers, sliced
  - 2 green onions, sliced (for garnish)
  - Sesame seeds (for garnish)

Instructions:

1. **Cook the Chicken:**
   - Heat olive oil in a large skillet over medium-high heat.
   - Add the chicken pieces and season with salt and pepper. Cook, stirring occasionally, until the chicken is cooked through and golden brown, about 6-8 minutes. Remove from heat and set aside.
2. **Make the Teriyaki Sauce:**
   - In a small saucepan, combine soy sauce, mirin (or rice vinegar), brown sugar (or honey), minced garlic, and grated ginger.
   - Bring the mixture to a simmer over medium heat, stirring occasionally.
   - Once the sauce starts to simmer, mix the cornstarch with water to make a slurry and stir it into the sauce.
   - Continue to cook, stirring frequently, until the sauce thickens and becomes glossy, about 2-3 minutes.
   - If using sesame oil, stir it in at the end for added flavor. Remove from heat.
3. **Combine Chicken and Sauce:**

- Pour the teriyaki sauce over the cooked chicken in the skillet. Stir to coat the chicken evenly with the sauce. Cook for an additional 1-2 minutes until the chicken is well coated and heated through.
4. **Prepare the Vegetables:**
    - While the chicken is cooking, steam or roast the broccoli florets. You can also quickly stir-fry the snap peas or bell peppers in a separate skillet with a touch of oil if desired.
5. **Assemble the Bowls:**
    - Divide the cooked rice among bowls.
    - Top each bowl with a portion of the teriyaki chicken.
    - Arrange the vegetables (broccoli, shredded carrots, snap peas or bell peppers) around the chicken.
6. **Garnish and Serve:**
    - Garnish with sliced green onions and sesame seeds.
    - Serve immediately, and enjoy your delicious Teriyaki Chicken Bowls!

These bowls are versatile, so feel free to customize with your favorite vegetables or additional toppings.

Cheeseburger Pizza

Ingredients:

- **For the Pizza Dough:**
    - 1 lb pizza dough (store-bought or homemade)
    - 1 tbsp olive oil (for brushing)
- **For the Toppings:**
    - 1/2 lb ground beef
    - 1 small onion, finely chopped
    - 1/2 cup ketchup
    - 1 tbsp mustard
    - 1 cup shredded cheddar cheese (or a blend of cheddar and American)
    - 1/2 cup pickles, sliced
    - 1 tomato, sliced
    - 1/4 cup mayonnaise (optional, for drizzling)
    - Salt and black pepper to taste
- **For the Optional Garnish:**
    - Shredded lettuce (for after baking)
    - Additional pickles (for after baking)

Instructions:

1. **Prepare the Dough:**
    - Preheat your oven to 475°F (245°C).
    - Roll out the pizza dough on a lightly floured surface to your desired thickness, shaping it into a circle or rectangle depending on your preference. Transfer the dough to a baking sheet or pizza stone lined with parchment paper.
2. **Cook the Beef:**
    - In a skillet over medium heat, cook the ground beef until browned, breaking it up with a spoon as it cooks. Drain any excess fat.
    - Add the chopped onion and cook for an additional 3-4 minutes until the onion is softened. Season with salt and pepper to taste.
3. **Assemble the Pizza:**
    - Spread the ketchup and mustard evenly over the pizza dough, leaving a small border around the edges.
    - Sprinkle a layer of shredded cheddar cheese over the sauce.
    - Distribute the cooked ground beef and onion mixture evenly over the cheese.
    - Add another layer of shredded cheese on top of the beef mixture.
4. **Bake the Pizza:**
    - Brush the edges of the dough with olive oil to help it brown and become crispy.
    - Bake in the preheated oven for 12-15 minutes, or until the crust is golden and the cheese is melted and bubbly.

5. **Add Toppings:**
   - After baking, top the pizza with sliced pickles and tomato slices.
   - If desired, drizzle with mayonnaise for extra flavor.
6. **Garnish and Serve:**
   - If using, add shredded lettuce and additional pickles on top before serving.
   - Slice and serve the Cheeseburger Pizza hot.

Enjoy your tasty and inventive Cheeseburger Pizza!

BBQ Chicken Pizza

Ingredients:

- **For the Pizza Dough:**
    - 1 lb pizza dough (store-bought or homemade)
    - 1 tbsp olive oil (for brushing)
- **For the Toppings:**
    - 1 cup cooked chicken, shredded or diced (grilled or rotisserie chicken works well)
    - 1/2 cup BBQ sauce (your favorite brand)
    - 1/2 red onion, thinly sliced
    - 1 cup shredded mozzarella cheese
    - 1/2 cup shredded cheddar cheese
    - 1/4 cup fresh cilantro, chopped (for garnish)
- **Optional:**
    - 1/2 cup sliced jalapeños (for a spicy kick)
    - 1/2 cup sliced bell peppers

Instructions:

1. **Prepare the Dough:**
    - Preheat your oven to 475°F (245°C).
    - Roll out the pizza dough on a lightly floured surface to your desired thickness. Transfer the dough to a baking sheet or pizza stone lined with parchment paper.
2. **Prepare the Chicken:**
    - In a bowl, toss the cooked chicken with 1/4 cup of the BBQ sauce to coat it evenly.
3. **Assemble the Pizza:**
    - Spread the remaining BBQ sauce evenly over the pizza dough, leaving a small border around the edges.
    - Sprinkle a layer of shredded mozzarella cheese over the sauce.
    - Distribute the BBQ-coated chicken evenly over the cheese.
    - Add the sliced red onion (and optional bell peppers or jalapeños if using).
    - Top with shredded cheddar cheese.
4. **Bake the Pizza:**
    - Brush the edges of the dough with olive oil to help it crisp up.
    - Bake in the preheated oven for 12-15 minutes, or until the crust is golden brown and the cheese is melted and bubbly.
5. **Garnish and Serve:**
    - After baking, remove the pizza from the oven and sprinkle with fresh chopped cilantro.
    - Slice and serve hot.

Enjoy your BBQ Chicken Pizza, perfect for a delicious dinner or a casual gathering!

Meatball Subs

Ingredients:

- **For the Meatballs:**
    - 1 lb ground beef (or a mix of beef and pork)
    - 1/2 cup breadcrumbs
    - 1/4 cup grated Parmesan cheese
    - 1/4 cup fresh parsley, chopped
    - 1 large egg
    - 2 cloves garlic, minced
    - 1 tsp dried oregano
    - 1/2 tsp dried basil
    - Salt and black pepper to taste
- **For the Marinara Sauce:**
    - 1 can (15 oz) marinara sauce (store-bought or homemade)
- **For the Subs:**
    - 4 sub rolls or hoagie rolls
    - 1 cup shredded mozzarella cheese
    - 1/2 cup grated Parmesan cheese
    - 1 tbsp olive oil (for brushing the rolls)
- **Optional:**
    - Fresh basil leaves (for garnish)
    - Additional grated Parmesan cheese (for sprinkling)

Instructions:

1. **Prepare the Meatballs:**
    - Preheat your oven to 400°F (200°C) and line a baking sheet with parchment paper or foil.
    - In a large bowl, combine ground beef, breadcrumbs, grated Parmesan cheese, chopped parsley, egg, minced garlic, dried oregano, dried basil, salt, and pepper. Mix until well combined, but avoid over-mixing.
    - Shape the mixture into meatballs, about 1 1/2 inches in diameter, and place them on the prepared baking sheet.
    - Bake the meatballs in the preheated oven for 15-20 minutes, or until cooked through and browned on the outside. The internal temperature should reach 160°F (71°C).
2. **Heat the Marinara Sauce:**
    - While the meatballs are baking, heat the marinara sauce in a saucepan over medium heat. Once heated, add the cooked meatballs to the sauce and simmer for a few minutes to allow the flavors to meld.
3. **Prepare the Sub Rolls:**

- Preheat your oven's broiler on high.
- Cut the sub rolls in half lengthwise and brush the cut sides with olive oil. Place the rolls on a baking sheet, cut side up.

4. **Assemble the Subs:**
   - Spoon the meatballs and marinara sauce onto each sub roll. Make sure to distribute the meatballs evenly.
   - Sprinkle shredded mozzarella cheese and additional grated Parmesan cheese over the meatballs.
5. **Broil the Subs:**
   - Place the assembled subs under the broiler for 2-3 minutes, or until the cheese is melted and bubbly and the rolls are toasted. Watch closely to avoid burning.
6. **Serve:**
   - Remove the subs from the oven and let them cool slightly. Garnish with fresh basil leaves and additional grated Parmesan cheese if desired.
   - Slice and serve warm.

Enjoy your hearty and delicious Meatball Subs!

Breakfast Skillet

Ingredients:

- **For the Skillet:**
    - 1 tbsp olive oil or butter
    - 1 medium onion, diced
    - 1 bell pepper, diced (any color)
    - 2 cloves garlic, minced
    - 2 cups baby potatoes or small diced potatoes (about 1/2-inch cubes)
    - 1 cup cooked breakfast sausage or bacon, crumbled (optional for extra flavor)
    - 1 cup shredded cheddar cheese
    - 6 large eggs
    - Salt and black pepper to taste
    - 1/4 tsp paprika (optional)
    - 1/4 tsp dried oregano or thyme (optional)
    - 2 green onions, sliced (for garnish)
    - Fresh parsley or cilantro, chopped (for garnish)
- **Optional Toppings:**
    - Hot sauce
    - Salsa
    - Avocado slices

Instructions:

1. **Prepare the Potatoes:**
    - Heat olive oil or butter in a large oven-safe skillet over medium heat.
    - Add the diced onion and bell pepper. Sauté for about 3-4 minutes until the vegetables are softened.
2. **Cook the Potatoes:**
    - Add the diced potatoes to the skillet. Cook, stirring occasionally, for about 10-12 minutes, or until the potatoes are tender and starting to brown. You may need to cover the skillet with a lid for a few minutes to help the potatoes cook through.
3. **Add Sausage or Bacon (Optional):**
    - If using cooked sausage or bacon, add it to the skillet and stir to combine with the potatoes and vegetables. Cook for another 2-3 minutes to heat through.
4. **Add Garlic and Seasonings:**
    - Add minced garlic to the skillet and cook for 1 minute until fragrant. Season with salt, black pepper, paprika, and dried herbs if using.
5. **Add Eggs:**
    - Make 6 wells in the potato mixture using the back of a spoon. Crack an egg into each well. Sprinkle the eggs with a bit of salt and pepper.
6. **Bake the Skillet:**

- Sprinkle shredded cheddar cheese over the entire skillet.
- Transfer the skillet to a preheated oven at 375°F (190°C) and bake for 12-15 minutes, or until the eggs are set to your liking and the cheese is melted and bubbly. For slightly runny yolks, check earlier; for firmer yolks, bake a bit longer.

7. **Garnish and Serve:**
    - Remove the skillet from the oven and let it cool for a minute.
    - Garnish with sliced green onions and chopped fresh parsley or cilantro.
    - Add optional toppings like hot sauce, salsa, or avocado slices if desired.

Enjoy your hearty and versatile Breakfast Skillet! It's perfect for a family breakfast or brunch gathering.

Taco Salad

Ingredients:

- **For the Salad:**
    - 1 lb ground beef (or ground turkey or chicken)
    - 1 packet (1 oz) taco seasoning mix
    - 1 cup shredded lettuce
    - 1 cup cherry tomatoes, halved
    - 1 cup black beans, drained and rinsed
    - 1 cup corn kernels (fresh, frozen, or canned)
    - 1 avocado, diced
    - 1/2 cup shredded cheddar cheese
    - 1/4 cup sliced black olives (optional)
    - 1/2 cup chopped red onion
    - 1/2 cup crushed tortilla chips
- **For the Dressing:**
    - 1/2 cup sour cream
    - 1/4 cup mayonnaise
    - 2 tbsp lime juice (about 1 lime)
    - 1 tsp taco seasoning mix
    - Salt and black pepper to taste

Instructions:

1. **Cook the Ground Beef:**
    - In a large skillet, cook the ground beef over medium-high heat until browned and cooked through, breaking it up with a spoon as it cooks.
    - Drain any excess fat. Stir in the taco seasoning mix along with a splash of water (about 1/4 cup) if needed, and cook according to the seasoning package instructions. Remove from heat and let cool slightly.
2. **Prepare the Salad Ingredients:**
    - While the beef is cooking, prepare the salad ingredients. In a large bowl, combine shredded lettuce, cherry tomatoes, black beans, corn, diced avocado, shredded cheddar cheese, black olives (if using), and chopped red onion.
3. **Make the Dressing:**
    - In a small bowl, whisk together sour cream, mayonnaise, lime juice, taco seasoning mix, salt, and black pepper until smooth and well combined.
4. **Assemble the Salad:**
    - Add the cooked ground beef to the large salad bowl with the vegetables and toss to combine.
    - Drizzle the dressing over the salad and toss gently to coat everything evenly.
5. **Add Crunch:**
    - Just before serving, sprinkle the crushed tortilla chips over the top of the salad for added crunch.
6. **Serve:**

- Serve the Taco Salad immediately, or keep the dressing separate until ready to serve if you want to prevent the salad from getting soggy.

Enjoy your delicious and customizable Taco Salad, perfect for a quick lunch or a satisfying dinner!

Potato Wedges

Ingredients:

- 4 medium russet potatoes (or any starchy potato)
- 2 tbsp olive oil
- 1 tsp garlic powder
- 1 tsp onion powder
- 1 tsp smoked paprika
- 1/2 tsp dried oregano (optional)
- 1/2 tsp dried thyme (optional)
- 1/2 tsp salt
- 1/4 tsp black pepper
- 1/4 tsp cayenne pepper (optional, for heat)

Instructions:

1. **Preheat Oven:**
   - Preheat your oven to 425°F (220°C). Line a baking sheet with parchment paper or lightly grease it.
2. **Prepare the Potatoes:**
   - Wash and scrub the potatoes thoroughly. Cut each potato in half lengthwise, then cut each half into wedges (about 6-8 wedges per potato, depending on size).
3. **Season the Potatoes:**
   - In a large bowl, toss the potato wedges with olive oil until evenly coated.
   - Add the garlic powder, onion powder, smoked paprika, dried oregano (if using), dried thyme (if using), salt, black pepper, and cayenne pepper (if using). Toss to coat the wedges evenly with the seasoning mixture.
4. **Arrange on Baking Sheet:**
   - Arrange the seasoned potato wedges in a single layer on the prepared baking sheet, ensuring they are not overcrowded. This helps them crisp up nicely.
5. **Bake:**
   - Bake in the preheated oven for 25-35 minutes, turning the wedges halfway through the baking time, until they are golden brown and crispy on the outside. The internal temperature should reach 205°F (96°C), and the wedges should be tender inside.
6. **Serve:**
   - Remove the potato wedges from the oven and let them cool slightly before serving. They are great on their own or with your favorite dipping sauces like ketchup, ranch, or aioli.

Enjoy your crispy, delicious Potato Wedges! They're perfect for a quick snack or as a side dish with burgers or sandwiches.

Buffalo Wings with Blue Cheese Dip

Ingredients:

For the Buffalo Wings:

- 2 lbs chicken wings, tips removed and wings separated into drumettes and flats
- 1/4 cup all-purpose flour
- 1/2 tsp salt
- 1/2 tsp black pepper
- 1/2 tsp paprika
- 1/2 tsp garlic powder
- 1/2 tsp onion powder
- 1/4 tsp cayenne pepper (optional, for extra heat)
- 1/2 cup unsalted butter
- 1/2 cup hot sauce (such as Frank's RedHot)
- 1 tbsp honey (optional, for a touch of sweetness)
- Celery sticks and carrot sticks, for serving

For the Blue Cheese Dip:

- 1/2 cup sour cream
- 1/2 cup mayonnaise
- 1/4 cup crumbled blue cheese
- 1 tbsp lemon juice
- 1 clove garlic, minced
- 1/4 tsp salt
- 1/4 tsp black pepper
- 1/4 tsp dried parsley (optional)

Instructions:

Prepare the Wings:

1. **Preheat Oven:**
   - Preheat your oven to 400°F (200°C). Line a baking sheet with parchment paper or foil and place a wire rack on top of the baking sheet.
2. **Prepare the Wings:**
   - In a large bowl, toss the chicken wings with flour, salt, pepper, paprika, garlic powder, onion powder, and cayenne pepper (if using) until evenly coated.
3. **Bake the Wings:**
   - Arrange the wings in a single layer on the wire rack, ensuring they are not touching each other.

- Bake in the preheated oven for 40-45 minutes, or until the wings are crispy and golden brown, turning them halfway through the baking time.
4. **Prepare the Buffalo Sauce:**
    - While the wings are baking, melt the butter in a small saucepan over medium heat. Once melted, add the hot sauce and honey (if using), and whisk until well combined and heated through. Adjust the sweetness or heat level according to your preference.
5. **Coat the Wings:**
    - Once the wings are done baking, transfer them to a large bowl. Pour the Buffalo sauce over the wings and toss until they are evenly coated.

Prepare the Blue Cheese Dip:

1. **Combine Ingredients:**
    - In a medium bowl, mix together sour cream, mayonnaise, crumbled blue cheese, lemon juice, minced garlic, salt, black pepper, and dried parsley (if using). Stir until well combined and smooth.
2. **Chill:**
    - Refrigerate the dip for at least 30 minutes to allow the flavors to meld.

Serve:

- Serve the Buffalo Wings hot with celery sticks, carrot sticks, and the chilled Blue Cheese Dip on the side.

Enjoy your spicy Buffalo Wings with the creamy, tangy Blue Cheese Dip!

Chicken Fajitas

Ingredients:

- **For the Chicken Marinade:**
    - 1 lb boneless, skinless chicken breasts, thinly sliced
    - 3 tbsp olive oil
    - 2 tbsp lime juice (about 1 lime)
    - 2 cloves garlic, minced
    - 1 tsp ground cumin
    - 1 tsp smoked paprika
    - 1/2 tsp chili powder
    - 1/2 tsp dried oregano
    - 1/2 tsp salt
    - 1/4 tsp black pepper
- **For the Vegetables:**
    - 1 large bell pepper, thinly sliced (any color)
    - 1 large onion, thinly sliced
    - 1 tbsp olive oil
    - Salt and black pepper to taste
- **For Serving:**
    - 8 small flour tortillas or corn tortillas
    - 1 cup shredded cheddar cheese (optional)
    - 1 cup sour cream (optional)
    - 1 cup salsa or pico de gallo (optional)
    - 1 avocado, sliced or mashed (optional)
    - Fresh cilantro, chopped (for garnish)
    - Lime wedges (for serving)

Instructions:

1. **Marinate the Chicken:**
    - In a bowl, mix together olive oil, lime juice, minced garlic, cumin, smoked paprika, chili powder, oregano, salt, and pepper.
    - Add the thinly sliced chicken to the marinade, tossing to coat evenly. Cover and refrigerate for at least 30 minutes, or up to 2 hours for more flavor.
2. **Cook the Chicken:**
    - Heat 1 tbsp olive oil in a large skillet over medium-high heat.
    - Add the marinated chicken and cook, stirring occasionally, for about 5-7 minutes, or until the chicken is cooked through and lightly browned. Remove the chicken from the skillet and set aside.
3. **Cook the Vegetables:**
    - In the same skillet, add another tablespoon of olive oil if needed.

- Add the sliced bell pepper and onion. Season with salt and pepper.
- Cook, stirring occasionally, for about 5 minutes, or until the vegetables are tender and slightly caramelized.

4. **Combine Chicken and Vegetables:**
    - Return the cooked chicken to the skillet with the vegetables.
    - Toss to combine and cook for an additional 2 minutes, allowing the flavors to meld together.

5. **Warm the Tortillas:**
    - While the chicken and vegetables are cooking, warm the tortillas. You can do this in a dry skillet over medium heat for about 30 seconds on each side, or wrap them in foil and heat them in the oven at 350°F (175°C) for 5-10 minutes.

6. **Serve:**
    - Serve the chicken and vegetable mixture in warm tortillas with your choice of toppings such as shredded cheddar cheese, sour cream, salsa, avocado, and fresh cilantro.
    - Garnish with lime wedges for a squeeze of fresh lime juice.

Enjoy your flavorful Chicken Fajitas! They're perfect for a fun and interactive meal where everyone can build their own tacos.

Pepperoni Pizza Rolls

Ingredients:

- **For the Pizza Rolls:**
    - 1 can (13.8 oz) refrigerated pizza dough (or homemade pizza dough)
    - 1 cup marinara sauce (for dipping)
    - 1 1/2 cups shredded mozzarella cheese
    - 1/2 cup sliced pepperoni
    - 1/4 cup grated Parmesan cheese
    - 1 tsp dried oregano
    - 1/2 tsp garlic powder
    - 1/2 tsp dried basil (optional)
    - 1 egg, beaten (for egg wash)
    - Olive oil or cooking spray (for greasing)
- **For the Marinara Sauce (optional):**
    - 1 cup marinara sauce
    - 1/2 tsp dried oregano
    - 1/4 tsp garlic powder

Instructions:

1. **Preheat Oven:**
    - Preheat your oven to 375°F (190°C). Line a baking sheet with parchment paper or lightly grease it with olive oil.
2. **Prepare the Dough:**
    - Roll out the pizza dough on a lightly floured surface into a rectangle (about 12x8 inches).
3. **Assemble the Pizza Rolls:**
    - Spread the shredded mozzarella cheese evenly over the dough, leaving a small border around the edges.
    - Arrange the pepperoni slices evenly over the cheese.
    - Sprinkle the grated Parmesan cheese, dried oregano, garlic powder, and dried basil (if using) over the top.
4. **Roll the Dough:**
    - Starting from one of the long sides of the rectangle, carefully roll the dough up into a tight log or cylinder.
5. **Slice the Rolls:**
    - Use a sharp knife or pizza cutter to slice the rolled dough into 1-inch slices.
6. **Arrange on Baking Sheet:**
    - Place the sliced pizza rolls on the prepared baking sheet, spacing them a little apart.

- Brush the tops of the pizza rolls with the beaten egg to give them a nice golden color.
7. **Bake:**
    - Bake in the preheated oven for 15-20 minutes, or until the pizza rolls are golden brown and the cheese is melted.
8. **Prepare the Marinara Sauce (optional):**
    - While the pizza rolls are baking, heat the marinara sauce in a small saucepan over medium heat. Stir in dried oregano and garlic powder for extra flavor, if desired.
9. **Serve:**
    - Remove the pizza rolls from the oven and let them cool slightly before serving.
    - Serve warm with marinara sauce on the side for dipping.

Enjoy your delicious Pepperoni Pizza Rolls! They're perfect for a party, a family movie night, or a quick snack.

Garlic Parmesan Chicken Wings

Ingredients:

- **For the Chicken Wings:**
    - 2 lbs chicken wings, tips removed and wings separated into drumettes and flats
    - 1 tbsp olive oil
    - Salt and black pepper to taste
- **For the Garlic Parmesan Sauce:**
    - 1/2 cup unsalted butter
    - 4 cloves garlic, minced
    - 1/2 cup grated Parmesan cheese
    - 2 tbsp chopped fresh parsley (or 1 tbsp dried parsley)
    - 1/4 tsp crushed red pepper flakes (optional, for heat)
    - Salt and black pepper to taste

Instructions:

1. **Preheat Oven:**
    - Preheat your oven to 400°F (200°C). Line a baking sheet with parchment paper or foil and place a wire rack on top.
2. **Prepare the Chicken Wings:**
    - In a large bowl, toss the chicken wings with olive oil, salt, and black pepper until evenly coated.
    - Arrange the wings in a single layer on the wire rack. This helps the wings become crispy as they bake.
3. **Bake the Wings:**
    - Bake in the preheated oven for 40-45 minutes, turning the wings halfway through the baking time, until they are crispy and golden brown. The internal temperature should reach 165°F (74°C).
4. **Prepare the Garlic Parmesan Sauce:**
    - While the wings are baking, melt the butter in a medium saucepan over medium heat.
    - Add the minced garlic to the melted butter and cook for 1-2 minutes, or until the garlic is fragrant and lightly golden (be careful not to burn it).
    - Remove from heat and stir in the grated Parmesan cheese, chopped parsley, and crushed red pepper flakes (if using). Season with additional salt and black pepper to taste.
5. **Coat the Wings:**
    - Once the wings are done baking, transfer them to a large bowl.
    - Pour the garlic Parmesan sauce over the wings and toss until they are evenly coated.
6. **Serve:**

- Serve the Garlic Parmesan Chicken Wings immediately, garnished with additional chopped parsley and extra grated Parmesan cheese if desired.

Enjoy your flavorful Garlic Parmesan Chicken Wings! They make a great appetizer, snack, or main dish.

Sausage and Peppers Sandwiches

Ingredients:

- **For the Sausages and Peppers:**
    - 1 lb Italian sausages (sweet or spicy, your choice)
    - 2 tbsp olive oil
    - 1 large onion, thinly sliced
    - 1 red bell pepper, thinly sliced
    - 1 green bell pepper, thinly sliced
    - 1 yellow bell pepper, thinly sliced
    - 2 cloves garlic, minced
    - 1/2 tsp dried oregano
    - 1/2 tsp dried basil
    - Salt and black pepper to taste
    - 1/4 cup chicken or vegetable broth (optional, for extra moisture)
- **For the Sandwiches:**
    - 4 Italian sub rolls or hoagie rolls
    - 1/2 cup grated Parmesan cheese (optional)
    - Fresh basil or parsley, chopped (for garnish)

Instructions:

1. **Cook the Sausages:**
    - Heat a grill or grill pan over medium heat. Grill the sausages, turning occasionally, for about 8-10 minutes, or until cooked through and nicely browned. You can also cook them in a skillet over medium heat.
    - Once cooked, remove the sausages from the heat and slice them into 1/2-inch pieces.
2. **Prepare the Peppers and Onions:**
    - In a large skillet, heat olive oil over medium heat.
    - Add the sliced onion and bell peppers to the skillet. Cook, stirring occasionally, for about 8-10 minutes, or until the vegetables are tender and beginning to caramelize.
    - Add the minced garlic, dried oregano, dried basil, salt, and black pepper. Cook for another 1-2 minutes until the garlic is fragrant.
    - If the mixture looks too dry, add the chicken or vegetable broth to deglaze the pan and add extra moisture.
3. **Combine Sausages and Peppers:**
    - Add the sliced sausages to the skillet with the peppers and onions. Stir to combine and heat through for about 2-3 minutes.
4. **Prepare the Sandwich Rolls:**
    - If desired, toast the sub rolls in the oven or on a grill until they are lightly crispy.

5. **Assemble the Sandwiches:**
    - Spoon the sausage and pepper mixture into each sub roll.
    - Sprinkle with grated Parmesan cheese if using.
    - Garnish with fresh basil or parsley if desired.
6. **Serve:**
    - Serve the Sausage and Peppers Sandwiches warm.

Enjoy your hearty and flavorful Sausage and Peppers Sandwiches! They're great for a satisfying lunch or a casual dinner.

Chicken and Waffles

Ingredients:

For the Fried Chicken:

- 1 lb chicken thighs or drumsticks (about 4-6 pieces)
- 1 cup buttermilk
- 1 cup all-purpose flour
- 1/2 cup cornstarch
- 1 tbsp paprika
- 1 tsp garlic powder
- 1 tsp onion powder
- 1 tsp dried thyme
- 1/2 tsp cayenne pepper (optional, for heat)
- Salt and black pepper to taste
- Vegetable oil (for frying)

For the Waffles:

- 2 cups all-purpose flour
- 2 tbsp granulated sugar
- 1 tbsp baking powder
- 1/2 tsp salt
- 2 large eggs
- 1 3/4 cups milk
- 1/2 cup vegetable oil or melted butter
- 1 tsp vanilla extract

For Serving:

- Maple syrup
- Butter
- Powdered sugar (optional)
- Fresh fruit or berries (optional)

Instructions:

Prepare the Fried Chicken:

1. **Marinate the Chicken:**
    - Place the chicken pieces in a large bowl and pour the buttermilk over them. Cover and refrigerate for at least 1 hour, or overnight for best results.
2. **Prepare the Coating:**

- In a separate bowl, combine flour, cornstarch, paprika, garlic powder, onion powder, dried thyme, cayenne pepper (if using), salt, and black pepper.
3. **Coat the Chicken:**
    - Remove the chicken pieces from the buttermilk, letting any excess drip off. Dredge the chicken in the flour mixture, pressing lightly to adhere. Repeat the process for a thicker coating.
4. **Fry the Chicken:**
    - Heat vegetable oil in a deep skillet or Dutch oven over medium-high heat to about 350°F (175°C). Use enough oil to submerge the chicken pieces halfway.
    - Fry the chicken in batches, cooking for 8-10 minutes per side, or until golden brown and the internal temperature reaches 165°F (74°C). Use a meat thermometer to ensure doneness.
    - Remove the chicken from the oil and place on a paper towel-lined plate to drain excess oil.

Prepare the Waffles:

1. **Preheat Waffle Iron:**
    - Preheat your waffle iron according to the manufacturer's instructions.
2. **Make the Waffle Batter:**
    - In a large bowl, whisk together flour, sugar, baking powder, and salt.
    - In another bowl, beat the eggs and then add milk, vegetable oil or melted butter, and vanilla extract. Mix well.
    - Pour the wet ingredients into the dry ingredients and stir until just combined. Be careful not to overmix; it's okay if there are a few lumps.
3. **Cook the Waffles:**
    - Lightly grease the waffle iron with non-stick spray or brush with oil.
    - Pour the batter onto the preheated waffle iron and cook according to the manufacturer's instructions until the waffles are golden brown and crispy. Keep the cooked waffles warm in a low oven while you finish cooking the rest.

Assemble and Serve:

1. **Serve:**
    - Place a waffle on each plate and top with a piece of fried chicken.
    - Drizzle with maple syrup and add a pat of butter if desired.
    - Optionally, dust with powdered sugar and garnish with fresh fruit or berries.

Enjoy your delicious Chicken and Waffles! This dish is perfect for a hearty breakfast, brunch, or a satisfying dinner.

Classic Clam Chowder

Ingredients:

- **For the Chowder:**
    - 4 strips of bacon, chopped
    - 1 medium onion, finely chopped
    - 2 cloves garlic, minced
    - 2 stalks celery, diced
    - 1 medium carrot, diced
    - 3 tbsp all-purpose flour
    - 2 cups chicken broth (or clam juice if available)
    - 2 cups milk
    - 1 cup heavy cream
    - 2 (6.5 oz) cans chopped clams, with their juice
    - 2 medium potatoes, peeled and diced
    - 1 tsp dried thyme
    - 1 bay leaf
    - Salt and black pepper to taste
    - Fresh parsley, chopped (for garnish)
    - Oyster crackers or crusty bread (for serving)

Instructions:

1. **Cook the Bacon:**
    - In a large pot or Dutch oven, cook the chopped bacon over medium heat until crispy. Remove the bacon with a slotted spoon and drain on paper towels. Leave about 1-2 tablespoons of bacon fat in the pot.
2. **Sauté Vegetables:**
    - Add the chopped onion, garlic, celery, and carrot to the pot. Sauté over medium heat for about 5-7 minutes, or until the vegetables are tender and the onion is translucent.
3. **Add Flour:**
    - Stir in the flour and cook for 1-2 minutes to create a roux, which will help thicken the chowder. Stir frequently to prevent burning.
4. **Add Broth and Liquids:**
    - Gradually whisk in the chicken broth (or clam juice) and bring to a simmer. Cook for about 5 minutes, or until slightly thickened.
    - Stir in the milk and heavy cream. Bring the mixture back to a simmer.
5. **Add Clams and Potatoes:**
    - Stir in the chopped clams with their juice, diced potatoes, dried thyme, and bay leaf. Simmer for about 15-20 minutes, or until the potatoes are tender and the chowder has thickened. Stir occasionally.

6. **Season and Garnish:**
    - Remove the bay leaf. Season the chowder with salt and black pepper to taste.
    - Stir in the cooked bacon and garnish with chopped fresh parsley.
7. **Serve:**
    - Ladle the clam chowder into bowls and serve hot, with oyster crackers or crusty bread on the side.

Enjoy your comforting and delicious Classic Clam Chowder! It's perfect for a cozy meal on a chilly day.